£1.00

GCSE Bitesize

D0784987

Drama

Complete Revision and Practice

Andy Kempe, Chloe Newman, Bev Roblin

Published by Educational Publishers LLP trading as BBC Active, Edinburgh Gate, Harlow, Essex, CM20 2JE, England

BBC logo © BBC 1996. BBC and BBC Active are trademarks of the British Broadcasting Corporation.

First published 2006; revised edition 2010, Fourth impression 2015

ISBN 978-1-4066-5438-7

Illustrated by Philip Hood

Printed in Great Britain by Ashford Colour Press Ltd.

Minimum recommended system requirements
PC: Windows(r), XP sp2, Pentium 4 1 GHz processor (2 GHz for Vista), 512 MB of RAM (1 GB for Windows Vista), 1 GB of free hard disk space, CD-ROM drive 16x, 16 bit colour monitor set at 1024 x 768 pixels resolution
MAC: Mac OS X 10.3.9 or higher, G4 processor at 1 GHz or faster, 512 MB RAM, 1 GB free space (or 10% of drive capacity, whichever is higher), Microsoft Internet Explorer® 6.1 SP2 or Macintosh Safari™ 1.3, Adobe Flash® Player 9 or higher, Adobe Reader® 7 or higher, Headphones recommended

If you experiencing difficulty in launching the enclosed CD-ROM, or in accessing content, please review the following notes:
1 Ensure your computer meets the minimum requirements. Faster machines will improve performance.
2 If the CD does not automatically open, Windows users should open 'My Computer', double-click on the CD icon, then the file named 'launcher.exe'. Macintosh users should double-click on the CD icon, then 'launcher.osx'
Please note: the eDesktop Revision Planner is provided as-is and cannot be supported.
For other technical support, visit the following address for articles which may help resolve your issues:
http://centraal.uk.knowledgebox.com/kbase/

If you cannot find information which helps you to resolve your particular issue, please email: Digital.Support@pearson.com.
Please include the following information in your mail:
- Your name and daytime telephone number.
- ISBN of the product (found on the packaging.)
- Details of the problem you are experienci   etc.
- Details of your computer (operating syste

X400 000002 3953

Contents

Drama from other times and places

Setting the scene for studying drama

Studying play scripts

The GCSE exam

Questions and answers

* Only available in the CD-ROM version of the book.

Introduction

Begin with the CD-ROM. There are five easy steps to using the CD-ROM – and to creating your own personal revision programme. Follow these steps and you'll be fully prepared for the exam without wasting time on areas you already know.

Topic checker	**Step 1: Check**

The Topic checker will help you figure out what you know – and what you need to revise.

Revision planner	**Step 2: Plan**

When you know which topics you need to revise, enter them into the handy Revision planner. You'll get a daily reminder to make sure you're on track.

Step 3: Revise

From the Topic checker, you can go straight to the topic pages that contain all the facts you need to know.

- Give yourself the edge with the Web*Bite* buttons. These link directly to the relevant section on the BBC Bitesize Revision website.

- Audio*Bite* buttons let you listen to more about the topic to boost your knowledge even further. *

Step 4: Practise

Check your understanding by answering the Practice questions. Click on each question to see the correct answer.

Step 5: Exam

Are you ready for the exam? Exam*Bite* buttons take you to an exam question on the topics you've just revised. *

* Not all subjects contain these features, depending on their exam requirements.

Useful websites

www.vam.ac.uk

The Theatre Museum is based in London. This site will tell you about their extensive collection of archive materials and objects, projects, exhibitions and how to use their facilities for your own research.

www.rsc.org.uk

There is a really helpful online guide to Shakespeare's plays on this site featuring synopses of the stories, character outlines, tips for directing, interviews with actors and some excellent production photographs.

www.thestage.co.uk

Use this site to find out what plays are being performed in your area and elsewhere. The site is also a useful source of reviews.

www.theatrenet.com

This site offers helpful links to different theatres and has a particularly useful news archive through which you can look up articles about plays, actors, directors, and so on.

www.shakespeares-globe.org

Take a virtual tour of Shakespeare's Globe Theatre on this site. There are loads of well-presented materials about Shakespeare, his plays and performances at The Globe.

www.doollee.com

This site boasts that it has notes on 13 000 modern playwrights and their plays. It is a useful quick reference guide.

www.bbc.co.uk/coventry/content/rich_media/shakespeare_game.shtml

This game is fun to play and will be a good piece of light-hearted revision for you.

www.bbc.co.uk/drama

This site gives details about current and recent television and radio drama productions.

www.ald.org.uk/gallery.php

ALD stands for the Association of Lighting Designers. Check out the Gallery on this site for some truly inspirational images of productions.

Acknowledgements

Film Cafe/Pentabus Theatre p. x (*Underland*); MARY EVANS/EDWIN WALLACE p. 4 (Pageant wagon); Pieter Jansz (1605–47) p. 5 (*Commedia dell'arte* troupe); BBC/Moviestore Collection p. 5 (*Fawlty Towers*); The Art Archive p. 6 (The Swan); The Art Archive/Army and Navy Club/Eileen Tweedy p. 7 (Portrait of Nell Gwynn); RIA Novosti/Lebrecht p. 10 (*The Cherry Orchard*); Robbie Jack Photography p. 12 (*Waiting for Godot*), p. 34 (*The Lion King*), p. 40 (both photographs from *The Crucible*); Moviestore Collection p. 21 (*King Lear*); Tristram Kenton/Lebrecht p. 32 (*Sweeney Todd*), p. 36 (*Shockheaded Peter*), p. 43 (*Blue Remembered Hills*); Simon Annand p. 38 (*The Caucasian Chalk Circle*); Stopwatch Theatre Company p. 45 (*Arson About*); Nils Jorgensen/Rex Features p. 47 (*Billy Liar*), p. 49 (*Blood Brothers*); Everett Collection/ Rex Features p. 51 (*Death of a Salesman*); TAG Theatre Co., Glasgow p. 53 (*Dr Korczak's Example*); Mark Longworth/National Theatre Archive p. 55 (*Sparkleshark*); Roxana Gabor/iStockphotography.com p. 57 (*Stone Cold*); Ken McKay/Rex Features p. 75 (*War Horse*)

About GSCE Drama

- GCSE Drama involves making, performing and critically evaluating drama you have read, seen and been practically involved with.

- You can specialise in particular areas of practical work.

Exploring themes and issues

Drama is a way of exploring and gaining new insights into the world of human thought and feeling and communicating these to an audience. Whichever board you are taking your GCSE Drama with, you can expect to:

- explore a range of different stimuli such as poems, news items, pictures, music, and so on, through practical drama

- use a number of strategies and techniques such as hot-seating, tableaux, thought-tracking, role play, and so on, in your practical exploration

- devise and script your own drama to convey your thoughts and feelings about the different themes and issues that have emerged from your practical exploration.

study hint >>

Always keep your eyes and ears open for things that you think might make good starting points for dramatic exploration.

Exploring process and product

The play that an audience sees on stage is just the tip of a massive iceberg! Most writers throw away far more than they ever publish, having tried out ideas and realised most don't really work. Designers make sketches, diagrams, pictures and models before finally producing what appears on stage. Actors and directors spend a lot of time 'workshopping' ideas trying to find the best way to play characters and make scenes 'feel right'. Whichever board you are taking your GCSE Drama with, you can expect to:

- explore the different elements that make up a performance, e.g. the use of voice, movement and gesture

- learn about the way set and costume design, lighting and sound, and so on, communicate meaning to an audience

- record the way your ideas and knowledge have developed and evaluate your own and other people's work.

study hint >>

Take risks, try things out, and be prepared to learn from things that don't work out the first time.

Exploring context and content

GCSE Drama tends only to look at a very small part of the wide world of drama and theatre. Even so, you can expect to:

- learn about drama from different times and places

- explore how drama reflects the times in which it was made and first performed and how the way an audience responds to theatre changes depending on when and where they see it

- consider what you think of as effective and important drama and why.

study hint >>

Make notes in your 'working notebook' about how you are linking different ideas, experiences and knowledge together.

Exploring plays

Exploring plays

- explore the storyline, themes and characters of plays written by professional playwrights

- go and see a number of plays and review them

- learn about how plays are made and what is involved in taking them from page to stage.

study hint >>

The more plays you read and go to see the more your understanding and appreciation of drama will grow.

The working notebook

Use a hard copy or electronic notebook to:

- record what you did in drama sessions and what your thoughts and feelings about the sessions were

- jot down ideas about roles you are developing

- make sketches and diagrams for costume and set design

- keep notes on plays you are studying and performances you have seen

- record what different drama techniques and explorative strategies you have used

- jot down questions raised for you by your work in drama and notes on things you want to find out more about.

study hint >>

The 'working notebook' is for you. See it as a personal diary and friend.

Keeping your working notebook or electronic record up to date will give you lots of material to include in your coursework and write about in your examination.

The art form of drama

- Drama communicates meaning to an audience through a number of different auditory (sound) and visual signs.

- The study of sign systems is called 'semiotics'.

Signs in drama

Drama occurs in time and space. It has to happen somewhere (space) and it takes a certain amount of time. The table on the opposite page shows the different signs that might work together to create and communicate meaning in drama.

Not every piece of drama uses all of the signs. For example, classical mime artists don't speak or make vocal noises (though some contemporary mime companies do). Radio drama uses no visual signs. By contrast, some dramas make particular use of locations. 'Site-specific theatre', for example, might take place in a real castle, the local allotment or even an underground lake!

Underland by Pentabus Theatre

>> practice questions

Once a piece of drama is over, it is over forever. Even if a performance is recorded, when the recording is played back the experience can not be exactly the same. Why not? What sort of things will have changed?

Signs communicated by the actor	Auditory signs – sounds that communicate meaning	Choice of words and vocal expressions (e.g. ummm, ah, oooh!): tone of voice volume pitch pace timbre	These signs communicate meaning in a given time.
	Visual signs – what an audience sees that communicates meaning	Physical appearance – how the actor looks: costume make-up / mask hairstyle What the actor does: movement gesture facial expression position on stage Physical appearance of the performance space: set layout furniture lighting projections	These signs need time and space to communicate their meaning.
Signs communicated by other means	Auditory signs – sounds that communicate meaning	Music Sound effects	These signs communicate meaning in a given time.

Topic checker

 Go through these questions after you've revised a group of topics, putting a tick if you know the answer.

 You can check your answers on the opposite page.

1	How would you describe a satyr in Greek drama?	
2	Can you name a Greek or Roman playwright?	
3	Can you name any *Commedia dell'arte* characters?	
4	Why did London playhouses close down in 1642?	
5	What is 'naturalism'?	
6	What is 'theatre of the absurd'?	
7	What are 'flats'?	
8	What is 'proxemics'?	
9	What is 'pathetic fallacy'?	
10	What is a 'thrust' or 'open stage'?	
11	What is a 'tableau'?	
12	What is 'cross-fading'?	
13	How can sound effects add meaning to a production?	
14	What kinds of things might an actor's costume reveal to the audience?	
15	What is the difference between 'straight make-up' and 'character make-up'?	
16	What is one of the major themes in *The Caucasian Chalk Circle*?	
17	What is one of the major themes in *The Crucible*?	
18	What is one of the major themes in *Blue Remembered Hills*?	
19	What is one of the major themes in *Billy Liar*?	
20	What are some of the points you need to consider when reviewing a live performance?	

1 Satyrs poked fun at stories from Greek mythology, history and society.

2 Famous Greek playwrights include Sophocles, Euripides and Aristophanes. Famous Roman playwrights include Plautus and Seneca.

3 Arlecchino, Pantalone, Il Dottore, Il Capitano, Pulchinella

4 Civil War broke out in 1642. Playhouses were closed down, partly to stop the spread of plague, partly to stop spies meeting up with each other.

5 The term 'naturalism' is used to describe drama that tries to reproduce 'real' life.

6 This term describes plays that reflect the idea that nothing much makes sense.

7 'Flats' are pieces of painted scenery, made by stretching canvas over a wooden frame.

8 This term describes the way space is being used to communicate meaning.

9 This is when a human emotion is somehow reflected by a natural occurrence, such as the weather or landscape.

10 This stage juts out from a back wall so that an audience sits or stands on three sides.

11 It involves a group of performers adopting a frozen pose as if they had been captured in a photograph.

12 One (or more) lights is dimmed while another light (or lights) is brought on simultaneously.

13 They can add meaning to a production by creating mood, atmosphere, historical period and/or setting.

14 a) when a play is set b) where a play is set c) something about the character d) the play's genre e) aspects of the plot

15 Straight make-up enhances an actor's own features, whereas character make-up adds additional effects.

16 Major themes include greed, corruption and social class.

17 Major themes include ignorance, fear and revenge.

18 Major themes include cruelty, social exclusion and status.

19 Major themes include social conformity and challenging the existing order.

20 Some of the points you need to consider include the actors' performance and technical aspects, as well as themes and messages.

The origins of theatre I

Introduction

Most of your work for the GCSE Drama examination will concern plays that are written or devised, rehearsed and finally performed in front of an audience in **a specially designated space**. You should bear in mind that you are working in just one tradition in a much wider world of theatre. In fact, having someone actually write a play that is then performed by actors in a building especially designed for the purpose is very different from many of the forms of theatre that exist around the world today. Many of the writers, directors and designers that you will come across in your GCSE course may themselves have been influenced by theatre from other times and places.

Primitive origins

When: the Stone Age–the present

What happened?

>> key fact Drama is a way of physically representing experience.

Cave paintings around 7000 years old depict men dressed as animals re-enacting a hunt. Drama involves people pretending to be someone or something other than themselves (the performers) in front of others who accept the pretence (the audience). Primitive drama is closely related to ritual and ceremony. In some cultures, these rituals have developed into highly sophisticated performances involving dance, storytelling, masks, puppetry and improvised action.

study hint >>

Think about common rituals and ceremonies you know that involve people dressing up and behaving in a special way. How do these relate to 'drama' as you understand it?

The Greeks

When: 1200 BCE–500 CE

What happened?

The word drama comes from the Ancient Greek word *dran* meaning 'to do'. Drama was an important part of life for the Ancient Greeks. Plays were staged as part of the festival of Dionysus, the god of wine and fertility. Performances were in open-air **amphitheatres** that could seat up to 20 000 people. Greek plays used a **chorus** to tell and comment on the story. The performers used masks to show what sort of characters they were.

>> **key fact** Tragedies drew on stories from Greek mythology and history, exploring themes such as death, power and justice. Satyrs poked fun at these stories and at society. Comedies invited the audience to laugh at everyday life.

>> **key fact** Thespis is remembered in the term 'thespian', meaning 'an actor'.

key people Thespis is said to have 'invented' the actor when in one of his productions he had someone step forward and answer the **chorus** and so created the first stage dialogue.

Famous Greek playwrights include **Sophocles** (*Oedipus Rex* and *Antigone*), **Euripides** (*The Bacchae*) and **Aristophanes** (*Lysistrata* and *The Frogs*).

The Romans

When: 250 BCE–500 CE

What happened?

Roman theatre developed what the Greeks had started. The stories were often the same but they were told in a way that appealed to the Roman audience: the **tragedies** became bloodier and the **comedies** became ruder!

The Roman court did not allow the state to be mocked in the way the **satyrs** mocked authority in Greek culture.

study hint >>

Find out which Shakespeare plays retell Greek or Roman stories.

>> **key fact** Satyrs were replaced by pantomimes that featured masked, clown-like dancers.

key people **Plautus** is remembered for his knock-about comedies, such as the *Menaechmi*, which influenced Shakespeare's *The Comedy of Errors*. **Seneca** developed the five-act format (also used by Shakespeare) for tragedies such as *Oedipus*.

The origins of theatre II

Medieval theatre

When: 1100–1500

What happened?

After the fall of the Roman Empire, Europe sunk into what is referred to as the **Dark Ages**. The Christian Church was very powerful and it disapproved of the theatre. However, in the 12th century people began to re-enact **stories from the Bible**. These developed into **Mystery Plays** that were performed on pageant wagons that were taken around the town. Later on, **Morality Plays** such as *Everyman* appeared to **warn people** of the awful things that would happen to them if they didn't live good Christian lives!

Pageant wagon

Commedia dell'arte

When: 1500–1750

What happened?

Commedia dell'arte began in Italy. It involved highly skilled comic performers improvising **stories that mocked human failings** such as greed, lust and jealousy. The characters were always the same:

Arlecchino – stupid and always hungry (Arlecchino later became better known in England as Harlequin); **Pantalone** – old, lecherous, money-grabbing; **Il Dottore** – always slightly drunk and very boring; **Il Capitano** – a big-headed coward; **Brighella** – usually a shopkeeper who cheats his customers; **Pulchinella** – empty-headed and violent; he later became Mr Punch in British puppet shows.

>> **key fact** **Characters such as these can still be seen in modern comedies such as *Fawlty Towers* and *Little Britain*.**

Rather than using scripts, *Commedia* troupes would work from ideas for scenes (*scenario*) and build in comic devices (*lazzo*) and practical jokes (*burla* from which we get the word *burlesque*, which was a popular form of entertainment in the twentieth century).

key people **Carlo Goldoni**
(1707–1793) started his career creating scenario for *Commedia* troupes but saw that the actors were losing the skill of improvising new ideas all of the time. He began writing down all of the dialogue he couldn't trust the actors to invent. His plays include *The Venetian Twins* and *The Servant of Two Masters*.

study hint >>

Think about how Sir Andrew Aguecheek, Sir Toby Belch and Malvolio from *Twelfth Night* might be seen as *Commedia* characters.

1   In what ways are the following rituals and festivals related to theatre?

• a traditional wedding

• a 'prom' ball

• a football cup final

• a street carnival

2   Medieval Mystery Plays and Morality Plays sought to educate people by teaching them Bible stories and promoting moral values. To what extent do modern-day dramas try to do this? Do you think they should?

3   The original *Commedia dell'arte* troupes performed their entertainments in the street. What special skills do you think street performers need? To what extent would these skills be useful for any live performance?

Commedia dell'arte *troupe*

Fawlty Towers

World events

323 BCE
Death of Alexander
the Great

218 BCE
Hannibal uses elephants
to cross the Alps and
invade Italy

54 BCE
Caesar invades Britain

79 CE
Vesuvius erupts and
destroys Pompeii

1040 CE
Macbeth murders Duncan
and becomes King
of Scotland

1066 CE
Normans invade Britain

1400 CE
Death of poet
Geoffrey Chaucer

1450 CE
Gutenberg printing press

1492 CE
Columbus lands in
the New World

The theatre explosion I

- The growth of theatre in the sixteenth and seventeenth centuries reflected a new age of scientific discovery and exploration.

- As new ideas about the world and human nature emerged, new words and art forms were needed to communicate them.

Elizabethan and Jacobean theatre

When: 1550–1625

What happened?

In 1576, a carpenter and part-time actor called **James Burbage** built 'The Theatre' in London. By 1600, there were at least four other **purpose-built, open-air theatres** in London. Around one in eight Londoners, including **Queen Elizabeth I** herself, regularly attended performances. Many of **William Shakespeare's** plays reflected the public's fascination with **history, foreign places and ideas about everything having its place in the world.** When Elizabeth died in 1603 people felt less certain about things. Plays became darker in their themes and the stories more violent. James I came to the throne (the term *Jacobean* is derived from the Latin word for 'James').

>> **key fact** The great English poet Geoffrey Chaucer (d.1400) had a working vocabulary of 8000 words. William Shakespeare (d.1616) used 24 000 different words.

key people William Shakespeare wrote at least 36 plays, most of which are still regularly performed today. Other notable writers and their plays of the period include **Christopher Marlowe** (*The Tragical History of Dr Faust*), **Ben Jonson** (*The Alchemist, Volpone*), **John Webster** (*The Duchess of Malfi*), and **John Ford** (*The Broken Heart*).

>> **key fact** In 1642, Civil War broke out. Playhouses were closed down, partly to stop the spread of plague, partly to stop spies meeting up with each other and partly because the Puritans in government just didn't like the theatre!

study hint >>

Research into what new discoveries were made during this period. This will help explain the explosion of new ideas and the growth of language.

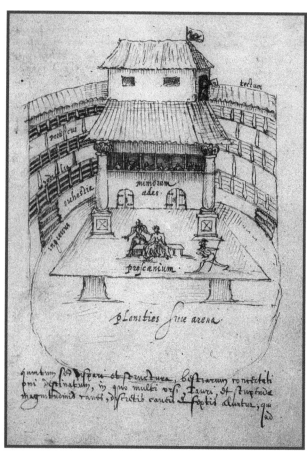

The Swan

The Restoration

When: 1660–1700

What happened?

After the **Civil War** and the execution of **Charles I**, theatres remained closed until **Charles II** was restored to the English throne. (The period that followed is known as **The Restoration**.) Having lived in France and enjoyed the theatre there, **Charles was keen to re-establish theatre in England**. Many of the plays from this period poke fun at the way rich people behaved.

>> **key fact** Women appeared on stage for the first time, notably Nell Gywnne, who became the King's mistress.

key people William Wycherley's *The Country Wife* is a comedy about Restoration society's obsession with sex. **Aphra Benn**, Britain's first famous and well-known woman playwright, is best known for her sexy comedy *The Rover*.

Portrait of Nell Gwynn

The theatre explosion II

World events

1400–1600
The Renaissance: massive interest in art, science and medicine; new lands, plants and animals discovered

1564
Birth of Shakespeare

1588
Defeat of the Spanish Armada

1599
The Globe Theatre built

1616
Death of Shakespeare

1620
Pilgrim Fathers settle in America

1642–1651
English Civil War

1660
Charles II restored to throne

1666
The Great Fire of London

1776
American Declaration of Independence

1789
French Revolution

1804
First railway locomotive

1815
Defeat of Napoleon at Battle of Waterloo

1817
First gas lighting in theatres

1829
First typewriter

1836
Samuel Morse patents telegraph

1837
Queen Victoria crowned

1839
First photographs produced

1865
Abolition of slavery in USA

1875
Alexander Graham Bell's telephone

1885
First modern bicycle

1895
First moving picture film show

Eighteenth-century theatre

When: 1700–1800

What happened?

Bigger and grander theatres were built in this time. Elaborate scenery was introduced on to the stage. The best actors became the stars of their day. People went to the theatre as much to be seen as to watch the plays – it was 'the place to be'. By the end of the century, some theatres had become so large that the actors had to bellow out their lines and adopt big gestures in order to be heard and understood. Audiences would talk, eat and drink throughout the performances.

key people Richard Sheridan wrote a number of brilliant comedies such as *The Rivals* and *School for Scandal*, while John Gay drew on the recently introduced form of opera in his musical play *The Beggar's Opera*. Well-known actors from this time include David Garrick, John Philip Kemble and Sarah Siddons.

>> **key fact** By 1794, Drury Lane theatre could hold 3600 people.

Victorian melodrama

In 1802, **Thomas Holcroft** staged a play called *A Tale of Mystery*. This launched a craze for plays that offered audiences a mixture of fast action, sentimentality and the idea that bad people always get their come-uppance.

>> **key fact** In 1800, less than 20 per cent of the population lived in towns, but by 1900, 77 per cent lived in towns. The population of Britain increased from 12 million to over 30 million during this period.

As the industrial revolution demanded more workers for the factories, people flocked to the towns from the country. Melodramas provided an escape from the noisy and dull routines of industrial life. In order to keep the audiences coming in, theatres had to keep offering new plays. As a result, a lot of the writing was poor and playwrights relied more and more on stunning special effects to keep the audience's attention.

key people **Dion Boucicault** wrote exciting plays that had amazing special effects. His play *The Octoroon* features a Mississippi steamboat exploding on stage. The famous melodramatic image of the heroine being tied to the railway lines and rescued at the last minute originates from **Augustin Daly's** play *Under the Gaslight* (though in this play it was actually the girl that rescued the fella!) Designers and technicians in Victorian theatres had to be very inventive as they were asked to stage horse races and sea battles as well as finding ever more ingenious ways of making ghosts appear and disappear!

study hint >>

A lot of popular films rely on special effects more than on a good story or good acting. Which ones can you think of? In what way are they 'melodramatic'?

>> practice questions

1   Shakespeare's famous character Hamlet says that the purpose of a play is 'to hold, as 'twere, the mirror up to nature.' In what ways do you think the development of theatre in Shakespeare's time reflected what was happening in art, science and world exploration?

2   In 1642 theatres were closed down for a number of reasons. One was that they made convenient places for conspirators to meet and plot. Another was that drama could be dangerous because of the questions the plays raised about society. Do you think drama can be dangerous? Should it be? Do limits and controls sometimes need to be put in place?

3   Imagine that you have recently moved from the country to a big industrial city in Victorian times. You work in a factory for 12 hours every day. Television, radio and film have not been invented yet and there are few places or opportunities to play organised sport. You can read but gas lighting is dim and expensive. In what ways could the local theatre add to your life?

Theatre in the modern world I

Drama can be performed on stage, television, film and radio.

Drama makes use of technological developments.

Eighteenth-century theatre

When: 1860–the present

What happened?

The term naturalism is used to describe drama that tries to reproduce 'real' life. Whereas melodrama is all about escapism and excitement, naturalism attempts to show life 'as it really is'. The English playwright **Tom Robertson** began experimenting with this style of theatre in the 1860s. His plays were called 'cup and saucer dramas' because he used real food and drink on stage in scenes that were recognisably 'everyday'. An example of a modern naturalistic drama would be *EastEnders*.

study hint >>

Consider the extent to which plays such as 'Blue Remembered Hills' are naturalistic.

>> key fact In naturalistic plays, it is as if the audience is watching other people's lives through a window.

key people The Russian playwright **Anton Chekhov** and Norwegian **Henrik Ibsen** both wrote plays which presented stories as if they were slices of real life. The great Russian director **Konstantin Stanislavski** worked intensively with his actors to try and get them to portray the emotional truth of the characters they were playing rather than showing themselves off as actors. In Britain, writers such as **Terence Rattigan**, **J. B. Priestley**, **George Bernard Shaw** and **Noel Coward** developed the form through the twentieth century until it became seen as the norm.

The Cherry Orchard

The power of politics

When: 1920–the present

What happened?

After the **First World War (1914–1918)**, a German director called **Erwin Piscator** developed a form of theatre that used film, photographs, banners and recorded voices. Piscator wanted to show that **things are the way they are because of politics**. This meant making the audience think about why characters in plays made the decisions they made and why situations were as they were.

>> **key fact** Since Piscator, many playwrights, directors and theatre companies have used theatre to show their thoughts and feelings about political issues.

key people A close associate of Piscator was **Bertolt Brecht** whose plays *The Caucasian Chalk Circle* and *Mother Courage*, as well as many others, had a huge influence on other writers and directors such as **Joan Littlewood** and **Augusto Boal**.

American realism

When: 1935–1985

What happened?

America quickly became world leaders in cinema after the invention of moving pictures just over 100 years ago. Hollywood, however, tended to be more interested in selling dreams than in exploring difficult issues. In the theatre though, writers such as **Tennessee Williams**, **Arthur Miller** and **Clifford Odets** were proving to be sharp observers of 'real life' and hard-hitting critics of the American dream that everyone can be happy, wealthy and free with plays such as *A Streetcar Named Desire*, *Death of a Salesman*, *A View from the Bridge* and *Waiting for Lefty*.

key people Director **Lee Strasberg** developed some of Stanislavski's ideas about acting into a technique known as the method. This basically involves an actor adopting the psychology of the character they are playing: if you believe you are the person then you'll behave like them!

>> **key fact** Actors such as Dustin Hoffman and Marlon Brando were trained in the method and have been successful on stage and screen.

Theatre in the modern world II

Theatre of the absurd

> **When: 1945–1960**
>
> **What happened?**

The massive destruction and madness of the Second World War (1939–1945) made a lot of people question the sense of things. The French writer **Albert Camus** concluded that all human existence was absurd. **Theatre of the absurd** is a term used to describe the plays written at this time that reflected the idea that **nothing much makes sense**. A good example is **Samuel Beckett's** *Waiting for Godot* in which two tramps spend all day waiting for a Mr Godot to turn up and save them from their miserable existence. He never shows up so they must always return the next day to wait again.

>> key fact The idea that life is essentially absurd had a particular influence on British comedy. In the 1950s, *The Goons* was a popular radio show that featured a number of Commedia dell'arte type characters in absurd situations. *The Goons* influenced *Monty Python's Flying Circus*, which first appeared on television at the end of 1969. By portraying the world as being somehow absurd, writers and performers are often able to make a serious point in a comical way.

key people In **Eugene Ionesco's** *Rhinoceros* the inhabitants of a town turn, one by one, into rhinoceroses, while in **N. F. Simpson's** *One Way Pendulum,* a character attempts to train a number of 'speak-your-weight' machines to sing the 'Hallelujah Chorus'.

study hint >>

Think of modern plays and television shows that are comical because of the way they show the world as illogical, strange or beyond a simple understanding in some way.

Waiting for Godot

Angry young men (and women)

In the 1950s, the director **George Devine** encouraged a number of new, young writers to put their work on at the Royal Court Theatre. One of these was **John Osborne**, whose play *Look Back in Anger* featured a character called Jimmy Porter, who angrily criticised middle-class values.

>> key fact The term angry young men started to be used to describe anyone who hit out at the establishment.

>> key fact Until 1968, plays could be censored for 'obscene' language or behaviour (such as nudity), or if their content was considered to be politically or religiously controversial. Since censorship in the theatre was abolished, playwrights have been freer to express their opinions and use the theatre to challenge ideas and beliefs.

key people Other writers to emerge in the 1950s and 1960s who were critical of the British class system were **Arnold Wesker** (*Roots, Chips With Everything*), **John Arden** (*Sergeant Musgrave's Dance, Live Like Pigs*), **Edward Bond** (*Saved*), **Shelagh Delaney** (*A Taste of Honey*) and **Ann Jellicoe** (*The Knack*). **Joe Orton** (*Loot, What the Butler Saw*) was a gifted writer of comedies.

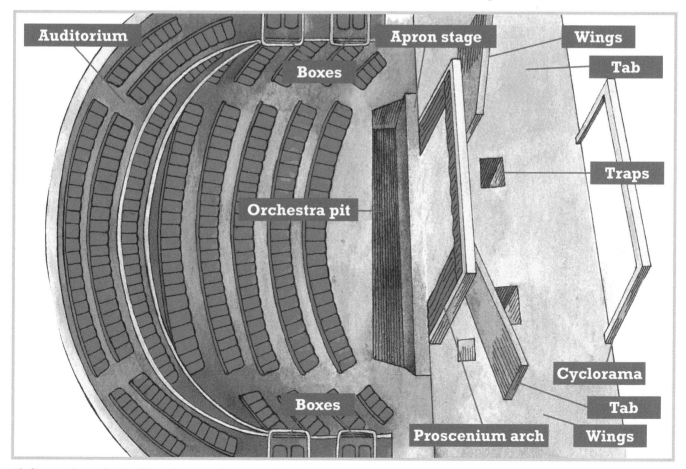

Bird's-eye view of a traditional proscenium arch theatre

Theatre today

- More people watch more drama than ever before because of the ready accessibility of television, cinema, video, DVD and YouTube.

- The range of different genres and styles of drama available today is greater than ever before.

- There are more people than ever before employed in the creative and broadcasting industries.

Drama in the twenty-first century

Some people thought that theatre would die out when film became popular at the beginning of the twentieth century. The same thing was claimed as more homes got televisions in the 1950s and 1960s. However, the number of people who regularly attend professional theatre in Britain hasn't changed much in the past one hundred years (around 2 per cent of the population).

>> **key fact** There are more people involved in amateur theatre than in amateur football in the UK.

>> **key fact** Mainstream professional theatre contributes over £2.5 billion to the UK economy each year.

Theatre cannot compete with film and television when it comes to size of audiences. Each year, over 21 million tickets are sold by professional theatres; compare that with the average audience for each episode of *EastEnders* of 15 million. However, it's important to remember that *EastEnders* is also a drama, as are most of the films you are likely to watch.

There is a healthy relationship between film, television and theatre. Attendance figures in the theatre rise when plays star actors known for their screen work. Some plays originally written for the theatre become successful films or television dramas (*Closer* by **Patrick Marber**, *Sleuth* by **Anthony Shaffer**) and vice versa (*Our Day Out* by **Willy Russell**, *Blue Remembered Hills* by **Denis Potter**, *Billy Elliot* by **Stephen Daldry**). Musicals that started in the theatre such as *Grease* and *Oliver* often go on to be box office hits in the cinema.

key people Major playwrights that have emerged over the last 30 years include **Caryl Churchill** (*Top Girls*, *Cloud Nine*), **Stephen Berkoff** (*Metamorphosis*, *East*), **David Hare** (*Plenty*, *The Permanent Way*) and **Sarah Kane** (*Blasted*). Much of the work of these playwrights has been hard-hitting and controversial, and contrasts with the popularity of musicals such as **Andrew Lloyd Webber's** *Cats* and *The Phantom of the Opera* or shows built around rock and pop music, such as *We Will Rock You* or *Mamma Mia*.

Companies such as **DV8**, **Theatre de Complicite**, **Frantic Assembly** and **Kneehigh** have been influential in introducing exciting physical elements to performance.

1 While it started in the theatre over 100 years ago, naturalism remains a popular form of drama. It is the form seen in most films and television series. Actual locations and expensive studio sets are used to give the impression of reality.

Watch a soap opera or popular television series carefully. How much like 'real life' are the characters and the situations? What does this tell you about naturalism as a form of drama?

2 What plays or musicals have you seen on film or television that started life in the theatre?

3 In December 2004, Birmingham Repertory Theatre had to close the production of Amardeep Bassey's play *Behzti*. The play had offended some members of the community so much that they rioted and the playwright received death threats.

Should drama be censored if it is likely to cause offense to some people? Who should decide?

World events

1903
First powered flight

1912
The Titanic sinks

1914–1918
First World War

1917
Russian Revolution

1926
First television broadcast
of a moving image

1937
First electronic computer

1939–1945
Second World War

1959
First microchip

1961
Berlin wall erected separating
communist Eastern Europe
from Capitalist West.

Yuri Gagarin becomes first
man in space

1968
Censorship abolished in
British theatre

1969
Man lands on the Moon

1973
Mobile phone patented

1989
Collapse of Soviet Union

2001
9/11 – terrorists attack World
Trade Centre in New York

Theatre words

- The word 'theatre' comes from the Greek *theatron* meaning 'seeing place'.

- A number of technical terms are used to describe what goes on in theatres.

- You need to know these terms and be able to use them when writing about your own work and performances you have seen.

Theatre terms

Auditorium	from 'audio' meaning 'to hear'. This is where the audience sits or stand to listen to and watch a performance.
Backcloth/ backdrop	a painted cloth that hangs at the back of the stage to give a scenic background. Backcloths are usually used in proscenium arch stages.
Cyclorama	a rigid canvas or plaster wall at the back of the stage. Lighting or projected images can be used on it to give a sense of space or sky.
Drapes	the curtains that hang on each side of a stage to mask the wings.
Flats	a flat piece of painted scenery made by stretching canvas over a wooden frame. Flats can be dropped onto the stage from the flies or moved in from the wings in grooves cut into the stage.
Flies	the space above the stage used to store scenery suspended on ropes so it can be dropped onto the stage.
Front of house	public spaces such as the auditorium and foyer. The term front of house is also used generally to describe all of the administrative jobs in the theatre such as selling tickets and publicising the play.
FX	an abbreviation for sound effects.

>> **key fact** An early sound effects machine was invented by John Dennis in 1709 to create the effect of thunder. Mr Dennis was upset though when his idea was used by another company and proclaimed that they had 'stolen his thunder' – a saying still used today.

study hint >>

Extra marks are awarded to candidates who use the correct terminology in their exam answers.

Rake	some stages are raked so that the back of the stage is higher than the front to help the audience see the action more clearly. The use of a raked stage gives us the terms upstage (that is towards the back) and downstage (closest to the audience). In many theatres, the auditorium is raked so that people sitting at the back can see the stage more easily.

The saying 'to upstage' someone means to force them to the back so that they are not noticed. When someone takes 'the limelight' it means they have pushed themselves forward so that they are noticed. This saying comes from the theatres of the eighteenth century when pans of burning quicklime were put at the front of the stage to light the actors.

Scenery	this term includes anything, such as painted backdrops, flats and furniture, which helps to give the impression of **a location**.
Set	the **three-dimensional environment** in which an actor performs. A set might be a very realistic representation of a living room, a dungeon or a part of a street. Sets can also be more abstract, offering different levels and types of spaces on which to perform.
Sight lines	imagine a series of invisible lines drawn between a member of the audience and any part of the stage. Ideally, every member of the audience ought to be able to see all of the action. Imagining these sight lines helps the actors and director check that they can.
Stage areas	stage areas are **defined from the actors' points of view**. So, stage left means that part of the stage that is to the left of the actor when they are facing the audience.
Trap	short for **trapdoor**. There are a number of different types of traps that are used for different effects but most are designed so that actors can appear or disappear very suddenly.
Wardrobe	where the **costumes** are made and stored.
Wings	the areas at **either side** of a proscenium arch stage that cannot be seen by the audience. More generally used to describe any **area in which the actors wait** before entering the performance space.

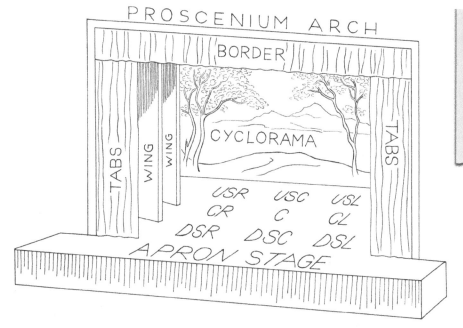

Positions on stage are taken from the actors' point of view as they face the audience e.g. Upstage Right, Downstage Left.

About acting

- Acting is at the heart of the art form of drama. It involves a person pretending to be another person and physically representing them.

- Sometimes actors can represent creatures, objects or even abstract ideas.

The craft of acting

Actors need to have **complete control over their voice and body**. They understand that even the slightest variation in the way they say or do something can affect the way an audience will interpret their performance. There are two views on how actors deal with this.

One theory is that an actor learns how to tune and play his or her body as though it were a complex instrument.

Voice	Body
tone	gesture
pitch	facial expression
volume	movement
pace	positioning
accent	posture

study hint >>

You need to be able to analyse and describe what acting involves – as well as being able to do it!

In this theory, the actor must remain detached from the character they are playing in order to communicate that character's feelings clearly.

>> key fact The French writer Denis Diderot summed up this idea when he said, 'Actors impress the public, not when they are furious, but when they play fury well.'

Another view of acting is associated with the Russian director **Konstantin Stanislavski**. In this theory, the actor works more from the heart and the head rather than the body by imagining themselves as the character and adopting their psychological and emotional reality.

While different actors may tend to favour one or other extreme, in practice, acting tends to combine both the psychological and physical, depending on the type of drama and the sort of character being played.

Acting terms

Ad-lib: this term comes from the Latin phrase ad libitum, which means 'as you please'. An ad-lib is **an improvised comment**.

Accepting: this word is usually associated with improvisations and refers to the way the improviser readily 'accepts' a fictitious situation.

Aside: an aside is a remark made **directly to the audience** as if the character is letting them in on a secret that the other characters on stage don't know.

Blocking: in **improvisation**, blocking is the opposite of 'accepting'. Blocking also refers to the process of deciding when and how characters should move, sit or stand in different sections (blocks) of a play.

Centring: this is a technique used by actors to find a way of showing a character physically. The idea is to imagine that the character is 'ruled' by a particular part of the body.

Character: it is characters' lines and actions that move the story on and make the points the playwright wants to make.

Characterisation: different actors and directors will interpret the same lines in different ways. Characterisation is **the way an actor decides to use his or her voice and body** to represent the character they are playing.

Improvisation: improvisation is when **actors make up the words and actions** rather than relying on a script. Some contemporary writers such as **Mike Leigh**, **Caryl Churchill** and **Ben Myers** have worked closely with groups of actors to develop plays from improvisations.

Pause/silence: when an actor pauses, the audience's attention is drawn to what they have just said and makes them wonder about what will be said next. Pauses give the impression that the characters are thinking which makes them seem more 'real' and **creates tension**.

Proxemics: the term used to describe **the way space is being used to communicate meaning**.

Role: the part an actor plays.

Stylisation: naturalism tries to imitate life as it normally appears to be. Stylised theatre, on the other hand, recognises that theatre is an illusion. Stylised characters may, therefore, appear to be **exaggerated** or **unreal**.

> **study hint >>**
>
> **Think of moments in plays when pauses and silences or the spaces between characters are used to create dramatic effects.**

>> practice questions

1   Choose a scene from a play you are studying. Make notes on how the way characters are positioned on stage in relation to each other (proxemics) could show an audience how they feel about each other.

2   Choose a speech from a play you are studying. Consider where you might place pauses in order to give the speech more dramatic impact or help an audience understand what the character is thinking.

The playwright's toolbox

 Play scripts are written to be performed, as well as to be read.

 Playwrights use a number of techniques that they know will engage a live audience.

Playwriting terms

Antagonist	the character who is in some kind of **conflict with** the main character or **protagonist** of the play: the Sheriff of Nottingham is the antagonist to Robin Hood.
Anti-hero	the main character of the play but may not be the sort of person the audience admires.
Chorus	usually, a group of people who are on the edge of the action. They **comment** on what is going on and sometimes provide links between the events taking place in the play. Sometimes the chorus might be just one person.
Climax/ anti-climax	the climax of the play is the most **tense** or **exciting** part. This doesn't mean though that the anti-climax is the most boring bit! Sometimes playwrights deliberately trick an audience into expecting something big to happen and then nothing does. This sort of anti-climax can create a comic effect.
Contrasts	good plays are full of different sorts of contrasts. Heroes seem more heroic if they have a villain to fight; sad scenes can seem more intense if they are contrasted with funny ones.
Dialogue	where two or more people are speaking with each other.
Direct address	when a character talks **directly to the audience**, such as in an aside. This sometimes involves the character treating the audience as if they are in some way a part of the play. At other times, it involves the actor coming out of role to comment on the play.

Epilogue	it's often used as a way of **summarising** what has happened in the play and giving the audience a few key thoughts to ponder **at the end** of the play.
Genre	a genre is like a **family**. Sometimes plays fit easily into one genre, such as tragedy, comedy, history, documentary or thriller, but sometimes they are a mixture and have elements from different families.
Hubris	overconfident pride accompanied by a **lack of humility** often resulting in fatal retribution
Metaphor	a way of representing something by **drawing a parallel** with something else.
Monologue	a speech made by just one character.
Pathetic fallacy	when a human emotion is somehow reflected by a natural occurrence, such as the weather or landscape.
Plot	the story of the play is simply the chain of events. Plot refers to **the way the story unfolds** and how the events are related to each other.
Positioning	where a character is standing or sitting. Playwrights will often use stage directions to indicate when he or she thinks the **physical position of a character** on stage is of particular importance.
Positioning the audience	the term **positioning** can also refer to how an audience is encouraged to think or feel about a character or situation.
Prologue	a **speech** made **to introduce a play**. It often reveals just enough of the story so that the audience is intrigued and encouraged to stay and watch the events unfold. A good example is the prologue to *Romeo and Juliet*.
Soliloquy	a speech made by a character who is **thinking out loud** as if no one is there to hear them. Perhaps the best-known example of a soliloquy is Hamlet's speech beginning, 'To be, or not to be. That is the question.'

study hint >>

Genre shouldn't be confused with style. Style is the distinctive way in which writers, actors and directors do things.

King Lear gets lost in a violent storm that seems to represent his troubled mind and emotions.

>> **key fact** In J M Barrie's play *Peter Pan*, the audience are asked to clap if they believe in fairies. This is the only way to stop Tinkerbell dying. Sure enough, the audience always claps; they have been positioned to do so as they understand that by not clapping the play simply couldn't continue!

Performance spaces

 Drama requires a space for performers to be seen by an audience.

 Different performance spaces have their own advantages and disadvantages.

Playwriting terms

Theatre-in-the-round: in a sense, this is the most natural sort of performance space. Whether it's a fight in the playground or the ritualistic presentation of a hunt in a tribal village, **an audience will gather round in a circle to see what is going on.** In theatre-in-the-round, there is a very close relationship between the performers and the audience. The audience may be seated or may just stand and watch.

study hint >>

The choice and organisation of the performance space will affect the way an audience understands the play.

Theatre-in-the-round

Amphitheatre

22

Amphitheatres	the Ancient Greeks built amphitheatres into hillsides having discovered that **sound carried well in naturally formed bowls** in the landscape. Some amphitheatres, such as Epidavros, could hold around 20 000 spectators. Amphitheatres allow every member of the audience to see and hear what is going on.
Thrust or open stage	a thrust or open stage is one that juts out from a back wall so that an **audience sits or stands on three sides**. This sort of stage can give the performers the same sort of close relationship with the audience as theatre-in-the-round, but also allows the back wall to be used to suggest different locations.

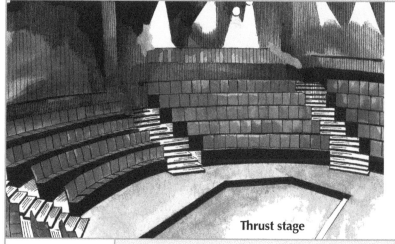

Thrust stage

study hint >>

The use of set, props and lights can also communicate meaning. Different performance spaces can limit the use of these.

Proscenium arch	this was introduced in the eighteenth century and is still often thought of as the most traditional type of stage. The effect of the proscenium arch is that the audience gets the impression that they are **looking into a picture box**, not unlike a television (see page 17).
Traverse	when a play is staged 'in traverse' the audience sits on **either side of a channel**. This sort of staging can give an audience the impression of being very close to the action, but it limits the use of scenery.
Promenade	in a promenade performance, the audience does not sit down. Rather, the performers work in different parts of the performance space and the **audience moves around** to see what is being presented.

study hint >>

Theatre involves performers communicating with an audience through the way they speak, move and gesture. An audience has to be able to to see what performers are doing and hear what is being said.

>> practice questions

1 What wouldn't you be able to do too much of in a theatre-in-the-round performance?

2 What sort of plays would work well in a proscenium arch theatre?

3 What sort of stage would you like to use for a production of a play that you have been studying? Why?

Drama techniques I

- Different drama techniques can be used to explore situations and issues.

- They can be used to create characters or investigate how characters think and feel.

- Some drama techniques can be used in devising and rehearsing plays.

Introduction

Throughout your GCSE Drama course, you will have been using a number of **techniques to explore issues, stories and characters in drama.** Many of these strategies have their roots in the sort of work professional actors and directors do when they are devising and rehearsing plays. Others have been developed by drama teachers to help students learn about the art form and how to use it in their own work.

>> **key fact** When you are writing about your work you need to be able to refer to these techniques in order to explain both what you did and how you developed your ideas and understanding.

Be specific

Just as children in different parts of the country often have their own special names for games they play or sometimes games have the same name but will be played slightly differently. The same is true of drama strategies. When you write about them, you need to make sure that you say a little about what the technique actually involves rather than assuming that the person who reads your work will automatically know what you mean just because you have written the name of the strategy down.

STRATEGY	PURPOSE	ACTIVITY
Conscience alley	To explore what a character might be thinking and feeling at a moment of crisis	Students form two lines facing each other. Someone representing a character in the drama walks slowly along this 'alley'. Each student says what he or she thinks the character might be thinking or feeling at a given moment in the drama.
Cross-cutting	To explore a scene from different perspectives	Cross-cutting means jumping from one moment to another in quick succession. It can involve moving backwards and forwards in time to show how a situation developed and what the consequences were. It can also be used to show how different characters perceived the same situation.

STRATEGY	PURPOSE	ACTIVITY
Essence machine	To represent physically and vocally the key elements of an idea or a situation	Working in small groups, students think of a line and an action linked to a given situation, character or idea. Then, they find a way of linking the lines and actions together so they can be repeated over and over in a mechanical way.
Flashback	To explore the background to a character or a story	Flashbacks can be acted out in different ways. The main point is to provide information about a character's past or something that has happened in the past in order to help explain something about the present situation.
Forum theatre	To explore the different ways a scene might be enacted or how a situation might be resolved	In forum theatre, a small group act out a scene watched by other students who can stop the enactment and offer advice to the actors on either what to do and say next, or how they might have done or said something differently to make it more effective. Sometimes it's useful if the student who stopped the action steps into one of the roles being acted to show what they mean rather than just explain it.
Hot-seating	To explore what a character is like and discover some of the possible reasons as to why they are as they are	One person takes on the role of a character in the drama. The rest of the group ask them questions about what they think and feel or about their lives in general. Sometimes it can be useful to hot seat different characters at the same time by positioning volunteers in different parts of the room. This can show that different characters have different perspectives on a given event or situation.
Imaging	To represent the ideas and feelings that lie beneath the surface of a character or situation	Imaging involves finding a way of showing something physically, and sometimes verbally. Rather than making a tableau like a 3-D photograph, this technique is used to show something that couldn't possibly be photographed, e.g. the idea of love or tension or perhaps what is going on in someone's head and heart at a particular time.

Drama techniques II

STRATEGY	PURPOSE	ACTIVITY
Narration	To provide either a background to a scene or give further information about a situation that would be difficult or unwieldy to act out	In narration, a performer provides a 'voice-over' to tell a part of a story or comment on a character or a situation. Narration can be a useful device to skip from one part of a story to another, e.g. if a group wanted to condense a fairly long play into just 20 minutes they might use narration to join selected key scenes together.
Role play	To explore a situation from the point of view of someone other than yourself	In role play, students imagine that they are someone else in a place somewhere other than the drama. The students don't necessarily have to change the way they speak and move. The main point is to examine people's attitudes and feelings when they are put into some kind of dramatic situation.
Soundscaping	To recreate the sounds and atmosphere of a dramatic situation or moment	Soundscaping involves using the voice and body to capture the different sounds associated with the atmosphere of a place or situation.
Split-screen	To explore different points of view or situations	Split-screen is two scenes showing different perspectives on a given situation, e.g. one scene might show how a group of boys gets ready to go clubbing and the other a group of girls. Split-screen is most effective when one scene freezes while the other activates then switches back again.

study hint >>

Too much narration can get boring. Audiences prefer to see action rather than hear about it. A narrator needs to be a good storyteller. They must sound interesting and engage each member of the audience as if they are talking to them personally.

study hint >>

If you use split-screen or cross-cutting, it is important not to jump too quickly from one thing to another or the audience may just get confused.

STRATEGY	PURPOSE	ACTIVITY
Tableau	To focus on what a particular situation looks like	Tableau is also called freeze-frame or still image. It involves a group of performers adopting a frozen pose as if they had been captured in a photograph. Tableau can be linked to thought-tracking in order to explore what characters are thinking, feeling or saying at a particular moment in the drama. Sometimes parts of a story can be represented through a series of tableaux.
Thought-tracking	To explore what a character is thinking and feeling at a specific moment in the drama	Thought-tracking is like putting a cartoon thinking bubble over a character's head. The drama is frozen and the character is asked to speak aloud what they are really thinking at a given moment. Of course, this may be very different from what they are saying, so the technique can help in the creation and understanding of believable characters.

>>  The plural of tableau is tableaux; so, one tableau, lots of tableaux.

>> practice questions

Think about the way you have used some of these techniques in your own drama sessions. In the table below, choose three techniques you have used. Give an example of when you used each technique and say how it helped you develop your understanding of a character, situation or performance skill.

Technique	Example	How it helped

Lighting I

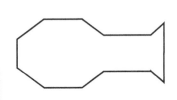 **Lighting helps the audience see the actors.**

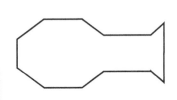 **It creates mood and atmosphere.**

Introduction

Lighting is quite a recent addition to the theatre. Performances from Ancient Greek times (1200 BCE) to Shakespeare's day (1600 CE) were performed in the open air in natural **daylight**. When indoor theatres were first established, **candles** were used to provide light. The first use of **gaslights** in the theatre was in 1817. These lights could be focused and made to shine with different intensity. In 1881, the first **electric** lights were introduced. These were much safer and more adaptable (and they didn't smell!). Today, a number of different types of electric lanterns are used to produce a huge range of effects.

Types of lanterns (also called lamps)

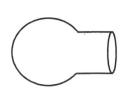	**Profile spot**
	A profile spot gives a strong, narrow beam of light that can be focused on an area of the stage or an actor. The convex lens in the lantern produces a circular beam but shutters inside the lantern can be used to give the beam straight edges.

>> **key fact** **The bulbs in household lamps are usually 60 to 100 watts. Most bulbs (also called lamps) used in stage lanterns are either 500 or 1000 watts.**

	Floodlight
	A floodlight doesn't have a lens so it can't be focused. Floodlights give a general wash of light. Sometimes floodlights are put together into a batten which can be used to light the cyclorama or act as a footlight at the front of the stage.
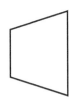	**Follow spot**
	A follow spot is a powerful profile spot set on a stand so that it can be moved from side to side and up and down by an operator. It is the sort of light that would be used to make sure a singer or comedian is always lit but can be used in plays to pick out important characters in key moments.

 Lamps and lanterns get hot!
Always use heat resistant gloves when working with lighting.

	### Fresnel spot
	The lens in a Fresnel spot is cut into a series of concentric grooves. This has the effect of spreading the beam more gently. Fresnels are used to provide a more general sort of covering light across the stage though they can still be focused to allow for different intensity.
	### Houselights
	These are the ordinary lights in the auditorium. There is usually the facility to dim these gradually in order to signal to the audience that the play is about to begin.
	### Par can
	Also called a beam light, the par can throws out a strong circular beam of light. It can't be focused but is useful for providing a strong, very theatrical effect (which is why it is often used at rock concerts!).

>> **key fact** **Stage lights generate a good deal of heat. Performers need to have some practice working under them in order to get used to this.**

	### Special effects lantern
	Special projectors can be used to create effects on stage such as moving clouds, rain, fire or psychedelic patterns.
	### Stroboscope
	Strobe lighting flickers to a set rhythm. Strobes can give the impression that the action is being slowed down rather like an old silent movie.

Lighting equipment

Barndoors

These are **metal flaps** that slot into the front of spotlights and help stop the beam spilling onto areas that do not need to be lit.

Cables

This is the correct term for the **wires** that connect lanterns to sockets and sockets to the control or dimmer board. Cables have a maximum load-bearing capacity – in other words, they can only carry a certain amount of **electrical current** before they get too hot and burn out.

 Cables should never be coiled when in use as they will get dangerously hot. They should always be coiled and stowed away tidily when not in use though, to avoid the risk of people tripping over them.

Lighting II

Dimmer (control) board

Dimmer boards allow the operator to **pre-set an effect** while another lighting state is running and **then crossover** by using a control slide. The dimmer board can also **automatically time** the fading of one set of lights and the raising of another as well as just flashing lights.

>> **key fact** **Modern dimmer boards are computerised so that each effect (LX) can be memorised.**

Gel

Gel is also known as cinemoid. A gel is a **thin, coloured plastic sheet** that is placed in a frame and attached to the lantern to tint the light. Different coloured lights are used to highlight the set and costumes, as well as create atmosphere. Some colours suggest certain things, for example, red can symbolise danger or bloodshed. Blue suggests night-time, while greens and purples can seem rather unnatural and spooky.

>> **key fact** **Shining a certain colour onto a piece of scenery or costume that is the same colour will not produce a good effect! Putting a strong red light onto someone dressed in red will simply make him or her look muddy.**

Gobos

Gobos are small metal plates that are inserted into a spotlight behind the lens in order to shape the beam and **project a chosen image** onto the stage or cyclorama.

>> **key fact** **Gobos and stage lamps are coated with a protective chemical. Touching a gobo or lamps with bare fingers will shorten their working life as the natural acids on human skin burn through the coating.**

Irises

An iris is a special **type of shutter** that is inserted into a spotlight behind the lens and is used to make the beam smaller.

Safety chains

Lanterns are clamped onto bars with G-shaped clamps but they must always be chained to the bar with a safety chain.

 Lanterns should always be secured with safety chains.

Blackout

The term used when all of the stage **lights are switched off** suddenly. Sometimes the effect will be to fade to black in which case the lights will be dimmed slowly until the stage is completely dark.

Cross-fade

The term used to describe the effect of one or more lights being dimmed while another light or lights are being brought on simultaneously.

Patching

Each lantern is plugged into a socket on the lighting rig. The wires from the sockets lead to another plug that is then 'patched' into a **dimmer rack**. Each socket of the dimmer rack is connected to a channel on the control board.

Preset

A lighting control usually has two rows of slides for each lighting channel. This allows the lighting operator to preset the lights for a second scene while the first scene is still running. When the scene changes the lights may be cross-faded or the first state taken to blackout and then the second state brought up.

Rigging

The **grid** that the stage lanterns hang from is called 'the rig'. Rigging is the term used to describe the act of hanging the lanterns in their required positions and focusing them onto the performance area.

State

This is the term used to describe what lights are on at any given time.

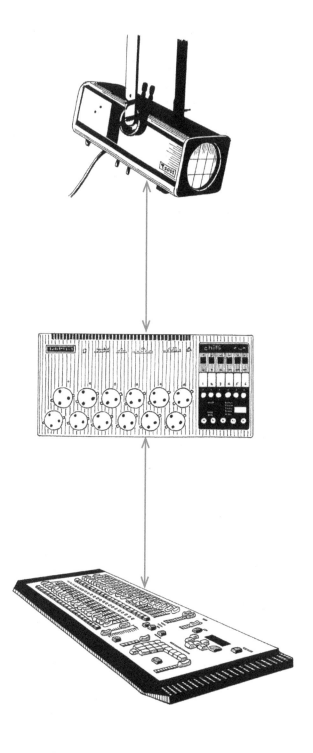

>> practice questions

1 Think about the way different colours affect you. Make a chart to show which coloured gels you would use to create different moods. Try to give examples of scenes from plays you have studied where these different moods need to be created.

2 Choose two or three pages from a play you have studied which would require a number of lighting changes and annotate them to say what sort of lighting effects you think should be used.

Sound

 Sound effects add meaning to a production by creating mood, atmosphere, historical period and/or setting.

 Sound effects can be live or recorded.

Live sounds

Some sounds occur naturally as a part of a performance, such as the words spoken by the performers, laughter, singing, screaming, or slamming a door.

>> **key fact** It may sometimes be necessary to amplify some of these sounds either to ensure that they are heard clearly or to add dramatic effect.

A scream might be deliberately amplified to shock an audience. A snore might be amplified to make them laugh. Laughter might be amplified and put through an echo chamber to make it sound maniacal. Ordinary domestic sounds, such as doorbells or telephones ringing, may need to be recreated on stage to give a sense of reality. These can often be produced live by wiring up real bells rather than using recorded sound. Similarly, radios and televisions used on stage can be fitted with controllable speakers.

>> **key fact** The direction a sound effect comes from is important. If a telephone on stage has to ring, then it is no good having a ringing sound coming from speakers placed at the back of the auditorium!

Sound effects can help give a sense of location. It may be theatrically interesting to have the performers themselves generate a soundscape.

Sweeney Todd

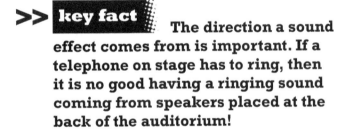

study hint >>

In a group, try to generate an atmosphere by recreating the sounds of:
• below decks on an old sailing ship
• an animal-filled jungle
• a scary wood on a wild night
• or a haunted castle.

Music

Music can have an immediate and **powerful effect on human emotions**. It can generate tension, a sense of sorrow or a feeling of fun and is often used to 'underscore' a scene; that is, the music is played in the background but nonetheless adds to the atmosphere.

Introducing a scene with carefully chosen music can place the action of a play in an historical context.

Playing carefully chosen music between scenes can add extra meaning to the action.

study hint >>

Think about how music has contributed to the films, television dramas or plays that you have seen recently.

Recorded effects

Comprehensive sound libraries are commercially available. These can be very useful for creating **background effects**, such as weather conditions, traffic or animal sounds, battles and fires.

>> key fact **Pre-recorded effects may need to be edited to the right length to suit your production. The BBC produce an extensive range of sound effects CDs.**

>> practice questions

1. Go through a script and identify all of the stage directions that suggest that a sound effect is necessary.

2. Think about what the actors are doing. Do any of their actions require sound effects that the playwright has not identified?

3. What ideas do you have for suitable music to open the play or fit in between scenes?

4. Plot the different effects onto a sound cue sheet showing the order they come in, when they should come on and at what volume, and how long they should play for (this is called their duration).

Costume

Introduction

Costume is **a way of communicating** to an audience the period when the play is set, the age, status, and mood of a character, as well as the style and genre of a play. A costume designer will collaborate closely with the director and set designer to achieve the overall style of a production.

What can a costume tell an audience?

The Lion King

① When a play is set

A sense of period is important in some plays. In *The Crucible*, the strict Puritan religion is reflected in the girls' costumes. Their outfits are designed to take away their femininity and to make them conform.

If you are designing a costume that reflects a particular period, remember that it is important to **research the era** to make sure the design is accurate.

② Where is a play is set

In some plays, costumes emphasise the **geographical location** in which the play is set. In *The Royal Hunt of the Sun* by Peter Shaffer, the costumes reflect the play's location in the Andes of the sixteenth century.

③ About the character

Costume can give an audience **information** about a character. Most of the characters in *Sparkleshark* wear school uniform but the way each has adapted theirs says a lot about them. For example, 'Natasha enters. She's fifteen years old and, although she's wearing the same uniform as Polly, her skirt is much shorter, the shirt is bright pink and unbuttoned to reveal some cleavage and her shoes are stilettos.'

study hint >>

Collect old photographs and use the Internet to gain a feel for a particular period.

④ The style or genre of a play

A director may use costume to **experiment with** the **style** of a play. Shakespeare's plays are often not performed in Elizabethan style costumes. In *As You Like It*, the costumes in Act 1 might be black and tightly fitting to symbolize the dark, restrictive atmosphere of the court, but when the characters arrive at the forest the costumes might be softer in colour and loose-fitting to show there is more individual freedom.

⑤ The plot of the play

Costume can be a key factor in the **development** of the **plot** sometimes, for example, Rosalind and Viola disguising themselves as boys in *As You Like It* and *Twelfth Night* or Malvolio's yellow stockings in *Twelfth Night*.

• Choice of colour is important. Some colours can look pale and uninteresting under stage lights. Always experiment before you decide.
• Colour can be used symbolically, e.g. black can represent death or a serious character.
• Check the colours and textures of the fabric work with the lights.
• Make sure you are safe and comfortable in a costume. Falling over a dress that is too long can turn a tragedy into a comedy!
• Dress to suit your character, not yourself.
• Check that your costume is suitable for quick changes. A slow costume change can destroy the pace or tension of a play.
• Work as a team – director, set and costume designers and actors – to make sure all your ideas fit together.
• Well-chosen accessories can put the finishing touches to a costume and will show an examiner that you have really thought about your character.
• Try and rehearse in part of your costume. It will help you get into character and you will also discover if it is suitable for the stage, e.g. does it restrict your movement?

Finish your costumes well. They can be your friends. They are your enemies if they are badly made and don't hold together.

Director, Ariana Mnouchkine

Make-up

- Make-up is used to 'paint' an actor's face and body in order to change his or her appearance.

- It can be used to create a special character effect, but it is also necessary to counteract the effects of stage lighting.

Make-up through the ages

The first recorded performer to use stage make-up was **Thespis**, the first actor to step out of the Greek chorus in the sixth century BCE. He used a toxic mix of white lead and red cinnabar!

The introduction of limelight made it necessary for actors to define their faces on stage.

The first 'greasepaint' produced in 1890 was a mixture of zinc white, yellow ochre and lard.

Since the 1940s, changes in stage design and developments in lighting techniques have meant that stage make-up has also had to evolve. Actors now have to take into account how the type and colour of lighting will affect their make-up.

>> **key fact** In the film and television industries, professional make-up artists are employed to prepare actors. In the theatre, most actors apply their own make-up.

Shockheaded Peter

Different kinds of make-up

❶ Straight make-up

This is when an actor **enhances** his or her own **features**. It consists of a base foundation, blusher to highlight and shape bone structure, and pencils to emphasise lips and eyes. The amount and type of make-up used will vary according to the age and nature of the character you are playing. Research into period is necessary: a woman in the 1950s would use a different style of make-up to women today.

❷ Character make-up

This will include adding **additional effects** such as:

- nose putty to change the shape of an actor's nose
- flesh wounds, scars, warts, etc.
- crêpe hair for beards and moustaches.

❸ Fantasy make-up

Often brightly coloured or containing additional substances, such as glitter, this can be used to create animals or fantasy characters from literature, such as the fairies from *A Midsummer Night's Dream*. It might also be used to suggest:

- inanimate objects
- emotions and moods
- monsters or aliens.

Fantasy make-up allows you to be as **creative** as you want.

 Always test for allergic reaction before applying make-up.

>> practice questions

Take a look at the following websites.

www.theatrelink.com

www.costumes.org

www.sfpalm.org (San Francisco Performing Arts Library and Museum)

www.cirquedusoleil.com

www.milieux.com

www.makeup-fx.com

The Caucasian Chalk Circle

 The Caucasian Chalk Circle is an example of 'epic theatre'.

 It aims to make the audience think about the decisions the characters make.

Background

Bertolt Brecht wrote *The Caucasian Chalk Circle* in 1944 while in exile in America. The rise of the Nazi party in Germany in the 1930s brought with it persecution and oppression. Brecht was in danger because he held Marxist beliefs and was forced to flee his native Germany.

Plot line

The play tells two linked stories, converging them only in the final scene. It is set in Soviet Georgia near the end of the Second World War.

The prologue allows Brecht to get across the moral of the story before the main action begins. It centres on two groups arguing over the ownership of a valley. Before the war, it was owned by goat herders and they argue that this precedence entitles them to own it now. The second group are fruit growers who explain how they can use irrigation techniques to convert 700 acres of infertile land into productive land. A delegate is sent to hear the case and he decides the fruit growers will make best use of the land. Even the goat herders agree! To celebrate this decision the fruit growers put on a play: *The Caucasian Chalk Circle*.

Both stories begin in a Caucasian city ruled by a governor who is killed by his brother. The Governor's wife flees the city leaving her baby, Michael. Grusha, a kitchen maid engaged to a soldier called Simon, takes the baby, hides him from the Ironshirts and flees. After much danger, Grusha arrives at her brother's house where she is forced into marriage with another man. Simon finds Grusha married to a man she does not love and with a baby. The Ironshirts take Michael away from Grusha and she follows them back to the city.

The Caucasian Chalk Circle

In the meantime, Azdak has been made a judge after saving the Grand Duke's life. In the final scene, he presides over the trial to decide whether Grusha or the Governor's wife should have the baby. After hearing both sides, he orders Michael to be placed in a chalk circle where both women have to attempt to pull him out to decide the winner. Afraid of hurting the baby Grusha cannot pull him and so reveals herself to be the more deserving of the two women. Azdak gives Michael to Grusha and dissolves Grusha's marriage allowing her to marry Simon.

Main characters

Grusha	simple, decent, unsentimental, working-class girl
Azdak	village clerk, appointed judge after saving the Grand Duke's life, a drunk with a strong sense of fairness
Simon	soldier, engaged to Grusha, an honest man
The Governor's Wife	shallow and selfish, has no love for her child, only her estates
The Singer	prime narrator of the stories, provides astute political comment

Major themes

The Caucasian Chalk Circle explores the themes of greed, justice, corruption, fairness and social class. Marxist thinking informed Brecht's view of society causing him to rebel against 'justice' that favoured the ruling classes. It explores the notion that resources should go to those who can make best use of them.

study hint >>

Look out for clues on staging and meaning in the stage directions that indicate a great deal about character, gesture, detachment, social justice, and so on.

>> practice questions

Create a storyboard for the whole play. Try to use just eight frames to tell the whole story – this means you will have to concentrate on what you think are the key moments. Give each frame a title.

Copy and complete the above storyboard. Compare your version with somebody else's.

The Crucible

- Playwright Arthur Miller makes a point about prejudice and injustice in 1950s USA by telling a story set in the seventeenth century.

- When working on *The Crucible*, you need to pay special attention to how Miller makes the audience feel about his characters.

Background

The Crucible is based on real events that took place in Salem, Massachusetts in 1692. In the small Puritan town where people's lives were dedicated to the service of God, several teenage girls were caught in the woods dancing round a cauldron. They were accused of engaging in 'the Devil's work'. Some of the girls fell ill and started to suffer hallucinations and seizures. Dancing was forbidden and the girls were terrified of retribution so they looked to shift the blame onto others. It was not long before the residents of Salem began to accuse other villagers of consorting with devils and casting spells. Old grudges and jealousies fuelled the atmosphere of hysteria. The Massachusetts government, heavily influenced by religion, put dozens of people in jail on charges of witchcraft.

>> key fact A crucible is a container in which metals are heated to extract the 'pure' element from dross or impurities.

Plot line

In Act 1: some village girls fall ill after being caught dancing in the forest, giving rise to rumours of witchcraft. Reverend Hale arrives and begins his investigations.

In Act 2: false accusations are made and all those accused are arrested.

In Act 3: Elizabeth and Proctor are arrested. Hale opposes and quits the court.

In Act 4: Proctor refuses to confess to witchcraft and to condemn the other accused. He is taken to the gallows.

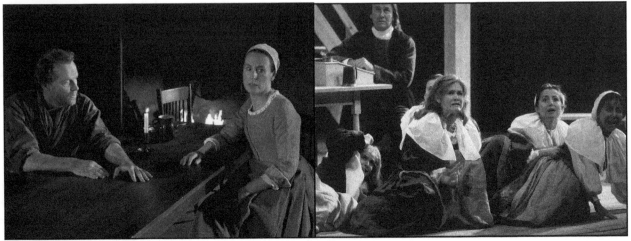

The Crucible

Main characters

Reverend Samuel Parris	pompous, unpopular and ambitious; talks of 'hellfire' in his sermons
Abigail Williams	a victim, but strong-willed and unscrupulous
John Proctor	the 'hero', decent and courageous, but had an affair with Abigail
Elizabeth Proctor	honest, devout and dignified; keeps to her faith
Reverend John Hale	proud of his knowledge and well meaning, but weak
Tituba	a slave, encouraged by the girls to carry out spells; confesses to anything when terrified
Thomas Putnam	a wealthy but greedy farmer who stands to profit from his neighbours' deaths
Ann Putnam	a bitter woman; seven of her babies died at birth, seeking someone to blame

study hint >>

Remember, this is a society in which manners and behaviour are very tightly controlled by custom. The characters' reactions are a response to the cultural inflexibility and religious pressure.

Major themes

'The Crucible' explores the themes of ignorance, fear, lies and revenge. The fear of witchcraft is endemic and based on an ignorant belief in magic, but the danger is real enough as the full might of the law is brought to bear on those accused of doing 'the Devil's work'. All the residents of Salem are afraid of being accused of witchcraft, some fear being hanged as a result, some fear the 'powers' of others. Parris fears for his reputation and his position as minister.

Many of the villagers hold powerful grudges against each other and use the pretext of the witchcraft trial to exact revenge on their fellows. Their spite has serious consequences. Abigail wants John Proctor for herself and plots to get rid of Elizabeth. Neighbours use the trial to settle old land disputes. Parris wants to shield himself from enemies he believes are against him.

Lies are told by almost everyone as they try to protect themselves and get revenge on others. The girls lie about their involvement with witchcraft, Proctor lies about his affair with Abigail and all the witchcraft accusations are lies. Finally, there is the 'triumph' of irrationality and superstition over sanity and reason.

>> practice questions

1 Make a list of subject-related vocabulary relating to voice, movement, gesture, and facial expressions. Then look at Act 1, from: 'ABIGAIL: Gah! I'd almost forgot how strong you are, John Proctor!' to: 'ABIGAIL: John, pity me, pity me!' How would you play the part of Abigail in this section in terms of voice, movement, gesture and facial expression?

2 Look at the beginning of Act 1. Draw a simple sketch to illustrate in the acting space where you feel characters could be positioned. Give reasons for your choices.

Blue Remembered Hills

 Dennis Potter was a leading writer of television dramas.

 On the surface, this play seems quite naturalistic, but Potter uses a number of devices to help the audience think about the underlying themes.

Background

Written in 1979, this play is set in the West Country in 1943. The characters are all children (poor, working-class and rural children) but adults play the parts.

Dennis Potter's decision to use adults to play the parts of children did not come from a desire for novelty or humour. He did not want to complicate the audience's reactions with any sentiment or sympathy they might feel at the sight of real children. He felt that real child actors would subtly censor their actions as children naturally do when under adult scrutiny. By using adults, the audience would be able to see and experience the actions and emotions directly.

The children aren't inhibited by the presence of any grown ups. It is a world of seeming innocence, but the innocence is shattered in a terrible climax.

Plot line

The action takes place during one summer's afternoon in a wood, a field and a barn. It follows seven children, all aged seven, as they play, squabble and fantasise, playing out their fears and hostilities. One character proves particularly vulnerable as the others gang up to taunt him and the play ends in tragedy as he plays his own, dangerous game of pyromania in a barn.

 key fact The play takes place in 'real time', with no flashbacks or other theatrical devices to alter time.

Main characters

Willie	easy-going, quite intelligent; uses his brain to counteract Peter's brawn
Peter	strong, inclined to bully, not very bright
Raymond	gentle, stammers, sensitive
John	fair-minded, looks after Raymond, challenges Peter
Angela	pretty, self-centred
Audrey	plain, wants to be Angela's friend
'Donald Duck'	abused by his mother; lonely and frustrated; not liked by the boys but the girls tolerate him and allow him to play with them

Major themes

'Blue Remembered Hills' explores the themes of cruelty, social exclusion and status. It shows how the characters struggle to establish themselves with their peers and how, if they fail, their insecurities can make them miserable and lonely. This pressure to conform and to belong can cause them to behave carelessly and even with cruelty to one another, especially to the weakest.

The play challenges our conceptions of the idyllic nature of childhood, the nostalgic 'blue remembered hills' of our own youth. It shows that childhood can be a fearful place, where emotions are deeply felt and social pressures enormous, especially from other children.

study hint >>

The characters are children and children behave differently to adults. Can you remember how you behaved at seven years old? Note the concentration and level of self-absorption that children exhibit.

study hint >>

Think what you did practically when you played a particular scene.

study hint >>

The stage directions are as much a part of the play as the dialogue. They are there for a reason. Don't ignore them.

Blue Remembered Hills

>> practice questions

1 Select a scene from the play that you have performed or explored practically. Make some notes on the character you played using the following headings: Type of Person, Relationship with Other Characters in the Scene, Voice, Body, Movement, Character's Objectives.

2 Look at the ending of the play, scenes 24 to 29. Write down your ideas on how the burning barn may be portrayed on stage. Pay particular attention to how lighting and sound can be used to create the desired effects.

Arson About

Background

Arson About is a fictional story but explores the very real issue of arson in schools. Its hard-hitting exploration of a contemporary issue means it works well as a piece of theatre-in-education, while the possibilities for imaginative staging makes it a good vehicle for young actors.

Plot line

Molly and Ian strike up a relationship but this is threatened when Molly's father, a fireman, announces that the family will be moving away. Molly meets Ian at the fairground. She is upset but doesn't get the chance to talk things through as they are joined by Stueey. After having some fun on the rides Stueey suggests they go to the school. He has been accused of sending threatening letters to one of the teachers and wants to find clues that will help him clear his name. Once in the school, Ian and Stueey start to muck about by throwing lighted paper aeroplanes around. Molly leaves them but gets trapped in a store room where she is suffocated by smoke as the building catches fire. The dead Molly witnesses the consequences of the boys' actions.

Major themes

On average, three schools are damaged by arson every day. The intention of the play is to show the human consequences when playing with fire gets out of control.

Main characters

Molly	loves her parents yet can get bored by and angry with them; likes to have fun but walks away when things get out of hand
Ian	likes Molly but is led by Stueey
Stueey	classmates might see him as a bit of a clown but teachers would see him as a disruptive nuisance; his childlike fascination with fire leads to the play's tragic ending
Shuttle	an outsider; Shuttle could easily be bullied or blamed for the spate of fires in the area – as it is, he is simply individualistic

Arson About

study hint >>

Don't confuse 'pace' with 'speed'! In the theatre, 'pace' is achieved through the creation of tension and sometimes this means slowing down the action.

>> practice questions

1   Make a list of the different places where the play makes self-conscious use of the magic of theatre. How does the use of this trickery help the play become more dramatic?

2   What importance does the character Shuttle have? If you were to direct the play, what would you want the audience to think and feel about Shuttle and how would you try to achieve this?

3   In Scene 7, 'Fireworks at the Fair', a number of rides, characters and locations need to be represented in quick succession. Describe how a small group of actors could recreate the fairground by using nothing more than their bodies, facial expressions and vocal skills.

Billy Liar

 Keith Waterhouse originally wrote *Billy Liar* as a novel.

 British writers became more interested in the lives of working-class people after the Second World War.

Background

Growing up in a northern industrial town in 1960, Billy Fisher longs to escape from his dull, cliché-ridden life. He invents a fantasy world and dreams of going to London to be a scriptwriter. He is engaged to two girls but is really closer to a third, a free spirit who represents escape. Billy's fantasies and lies catch up with him and he ultimately lacks the courage to break free from his hometown.

Plot line

In Act 1: Billy Fisher, a clerk in an undertakers, lies to his family, telling them he has been offered a job in London as a scriptwriter. He is in trouble at work for stealing post money and for some missing calendars. Billy plans to get back the engagement ring from Barbara, his fiancee, to give to Rita, to whom he is also engaged.

In Act 2: Billy struggles to keep Barbara and Rita apart. His father is not pleased to hear of Billy's engagement to Barbara but attempts to use this as a way into having a meaningful conversation with his son. They begin to communicate but soon fail under a combination of Billy's evasion and his grandmother's single-minded interfering. During the ensuing argument, Florence falls ill and the family get her off to bed. During a stand-up row with Rita, Geoffrey enters with the news of Florence's death.

In Act 3: Billy's boss, Mr Duxbury, comes to arrange the funeral and Geoffrey finds out about Billy's stealing at work, but Duxbury agrees that he will not report Billy to the police if Billy is sensible and pays back what he has taken.

In the front garden, Billy and Liz discuss their plans and dreams and it is clear that they share feelings for adventure, but for Billy they are all in his head. Liz and Billy decide to go to London together that night and agree to meet at the station at 11.00.

Back inside, Billy argues with his father about his plans to work in London and all his bitter feelings about his dull life come to the surface. He packs a suitcase and leaves… but the last thing the audience sees is Billy returning to the silent house, having failed to break away. He cannot leave for a new life in London and returns to his fantasy life at home.

Main characters

Billy Fisher	19 years old, imaginative and creative; wants to escape from his dull background; makes up stories and embellishes his life
Geoffrey Fisher	Billy's father, blustering, hard-working; exasperated by Billy
Alice Fisher	Billy's mother, simple but strong woman; her views on life are set and focused on appearances
Florence Boothroyd	Billy's grandmother, rambles to herself and daydreams; highly critical
Arthur Crabtree	Billy's friend; sympathises with Billy at first but grows impatient with him
Barbara	solid and dull, sees the world through rose-coloured glasses; engaged to Billy
Rita	simple, extrovert and raucous working-class girl; also engaged to Billy
Liz	closest to Billy in character; warm and generous; she transcends the narrow social boundaries that surround her

Major themes

The play examines the themes of social conformity and the desire to challenge the existing order. It contrasts the dull world of Billy's parents, where people dutifully work hard all their lives for few rewards, with the world that is in Billy's head. When Billy's fantasies spill out of his imagination into his real world, the consequences are both funny and moving.

study hint >>

The practical skills that an actor has at his or her disposal are voice, movement, gesture, facial expression and the use of the space provided.

Billy Liar

>> practice questions

1   What costumes would you choose for Liz, Rita and Barbara to show the differences in their characters? Give reasons for your choices.

2   Choose a scene you particularly like. Look at the dialogue and find where moments of comedy are used. Annotate the script to show how the humour works and the effect it has.

Blood Brothers

 This story is based on an old superstition that tragedy will occur if twins are separated.

 The play is generally naturalistic in style but uses a number of theatrical tricks to make it lively and punchy.

Background

Blood Brothers was originally written for a Youth Theatre group. The multi-award winning musical version has been playing in London's West End since 1988. In this play and other successful dramas such as *Educating Rita* and *Shirley Valentine*, playwright Willy Russell draws on his own experience of working class life in Liverpool to examine class differences, attitudes and prejudices.

Plot line

Mrs Johnston works as a cleaner for Mrs Lyons. She already has seven children when she discovers she is expecting twins. Her husband has left her and she wonders how she will manage. Mrs Lyons has no children and offers to take one of the babies. Despite Mrs Lyons doing all she can to keep them apart, the boys meet and become 'blood brothers'. The different environments in which they grow up lead them into different life styles. Mickey experiences work in a factory, unemployment and depression. Eddie has a great time at university and takes over as director of his father's business (the factory that employs Mickey). Their childhood friend Linda grows up with them and feels torn between them. She marries Mickey, but when he suspects she is having an affair with Eddie he goes after him with a gun. Mrs Lyons intervenes and both men are killed.

Main characters

Eddie	impressed by Mickey's adventurousness as a boy; becomes a charming, witty, educated and wealthy man
Mickey	a fun loving lad but as he grows up he struggles to express himself and feels increasingly worthless
Mrs Johnston	working class, down to earth, living with broken dreams
Mrs Lyons	quite wealthy; lives in fear of losing Eddie
Linda	friend to both Mickey and Eddie; marries one but loves the other

study hint >>

Lighting, music, sound effects, props and costumes can all be used to signal to an audience that time has moved on in a play.

'Blood Brothers' explores the balance between nature and nurture in the way our lives turn out. Mickey and Eddie have different lives because of the money and education available to them, but this doesn't stop them feeling a natural bond to each other. Mrs Johnston is superstitious and believes in fate; Mrs Lyons uses this to scare her and keep the twins apart. The lies that Mrs Lyons tells to keep the twins separate drive her mad. Is the ultimate tragedy fate, or the result of the decision the two women made in the belief it would be best for everyone?

Blood Brothers

>> practice questions

1   **Fill in a table like the one shown below:**

	Similarities	Differences	How an actor could show this
Mickey			
Eddie			

2   **Make a list of all of the different locations of action in the play. How might you suggest each location by using just a few props or stage furnishings?**

3   **In the last scene of the play, the tension needs to be built up to the point where the brothers die. The pace then needs to change as the narrator adds the epilogue. Write a set of notes to suggest how you might achieve the maximum dramatic effect by using pace in this scene.**

Death of a Salesman

- This play made playwright Arthur Miller and the character of Willy Loman into household names after its first production in 1949.

- It explores the idea of the 'American dream' in which anyone can become successful.

Background

'Death of a Salesman' is in many ways like a Greek tragedy, though its hero, Willy, isn't a god or king, but just an ordinary guy (a low-man) whose fault is that he doesn't know himself well enough and can't see the flaws of the society in which he lives.

Plot line

Willy Loman is an ageing travelling salesman who has had only limited success yet continues to believe that he just needs to get lucky. As he reminisces about better times the audience sees, through a series of flashbacks, how he has been driven by the idea of material success rather than spiritual happiness. He loses his job and his son Biff confronts him with his 'phony dream'. He realises that he is worth more dead than alive and kills himself by deliberately crashing his car.

Main characters

Willy Loman	obsessed with being rich and well-liked; is losing his grip on reality
Linda	Willy's wife; tries to protect her husband from the reality of his failure
Biff	Willy's oldest son; the 'all-star athlete' leaves home after discovering his father was having an affair, but ends up spending time in jail
Happy	the younger son who craves his parents' attention and blindly accepts Willy's dreams of success
Ben	Willy's rich and successful brother; he is dead in the real time of the play, but appears in many of Willy's memories

Major themes

Willy Loman represents all those men who struggle to support their families by working in a system (represented by his boss) which doesn't really care about them as individuals. Willy's tragic mistake is that he only sees success in terms of wealth and belongings. He has no spiritual values so when he loses his job he can see no point to his life. The play can be seen as a criticism of capitalism.

study hint >>

When designing a set, you need to think about the stage or studio space for which it will be built.

Death of a Salesman

>> practice questions

1   How would the actor playing Ben show that he is a part of Willy's idealised memory? Consider how they might move, speak and position themselves on the stage.

2   The action needs to be able to move from the Loman's house to Willy's idealised visions of the past. Design a set that would allow for these shifts of time and place, yet not require changes in scenery that would slow the action down.

3   Look at how Willy sees Biff in his memories and contrast this with how the older Biff comes across. What advice would you give to the actor playing Biff regarding how to change from Willy's idealised version of the character to the 'real' man?

4   Imagine that Biff and Happy meet up one year after their father's death and that Linda has also died. Write a scene which shows how they remember their parents. The dialogue should make reference to instances in the play to show your knowledge of the plot and characters.

Dr Korczak's Example

- The play is based on the true story of the Dr Korczak's orphanage for Jewish children.

- Brechtian devices distance the audience from the horror and brutality of the Holocaust in order to help the audience think about the play's issues.

Background

Janusz Korczak was an educationalist and well-known writer of children's stories. He believed that children should be respected and listened to and given the right to judge each other. The principles used to organise the orphanage he ran became the basis for the United Nations Convention on the Rights of the Child.

Plot line

The action takes place in Warsaw in 1942 when the city was under Nazi occupation and the Jewish population had been herded into a ghetto. Adzio has been living on the streets. When he is caught for stealing, Dr Korczak saves him from execution by taking him into his orphanage. He is taught the rules by Stephanie, but can't see the point of them as he believes they will all die anyway. At the end of the play Dr Korczak and the orphans are taken away to a death camp. Adzio and Stephanie, however, escape.

Main characters

Dr Korczak	loved by the children in his care, respected by both the Jewish community and the Nazis for his work
Adzio	streetwise, a fighter and survivor
Stephanie	has faith in Dr Korczak and his ideas, but her beliefs are shaken by Adzio's brutally realistic view of the situation

Other characters in the play, such as soldiers and orphans, could be played by actors, though in the original production they were represented by simple puppets.

study hint >>

Rather then trying to adopt Polish accents, consider how different tones of voice could be used to depict the characters.

Major themes

The play presents an argument. On the one hand, Adzio's philosophy is to fight violence with violence and survive at any cost. On the other hand is Dr Korczak's belief that evil must be resisted by setting an example of rational and humane behaviour. Although Dr Korczak was murdered by the Nazis, his principles have lived on. The fictitious characters of Adzio and Stephanie may have escaped the transport to the death camp, but whether or not they survived the Holocaust is left unkown.

Dr Korczak's Example

study hint >>

Research the ideas of Brecht and consider how these could be used in a production of the play.

>> practice questions

1 How would the actor playing Dr Korczak make his first entrance? Think about the way he would need to move and position himself on stage?

2 Explore how a variety of objects might be used as puppets. For example, try using shoes, hats, gloves and helmets to represent different characters.

3 As an actor, how would you communicate the role of Adzio to an audience showing that he has been hardened by life but is still, essentially, just a boy?

4 An audience may be deeply moved by the end of the play, but they should also be encouraged to think about Dr Korczak's legacy. Consider how you might present the Rights of the Child in a way that will make the audience think.

Sparkleshark

- The play was first performed as part of the National Theatre's New Connections project

- Philip Ridley grew up and still lives in the East End of London. He is well known for writing fantastical children's stories as well as gritty and violent adult dramas.

Background

Sparkleshark is set in a stark and menacing urban landscape. Many of the characters have adopted an identity they think will help them survive. Like the character Jake, Philip Ridley has always been fascinated by fantasy (and was bullied at school for this). However, he believes that storytellers can offer people hope and help them to tackle the terrors of modern urban life.

Plot line

Jake goes to the roof of his tower block to write stories. He is discovered by Polly who has gone to fix the satellite dish for her brother Finn. They are joined by Natasha and Carol, who call to some boys down below in the hope that one of them, Russell, will come up. Jake has been bullied by Russell, so when he arrives Jake hides behind the girls. Russell finds him and threatens to dangle him over the edge of the roof. Polly and Natasha try to save Jake by saying that he was telling them a story about a princess who, like Natasha, has been shunned by her father. One by one, all of the teenagers become involved in making up and acting out the story of how a handsome prince faces a number of challenges in order to save her. Even Finn, who everyone is terrified of, joins in and plays a fearsome, yet beautiful, Dragon called Sparkleshark. The story leads to the teenagers seeing each other in a new light.

Major themes

Sparkleshark illustrates the power storytelling has to teach us about ourselves and each other. The characters are stereotypes that could be found in any school: the geek, Little Miss Perfect, Mr Cool, the bully and his henchmen, the teen queen and her handmaiden. As the fairy tale unfolds, they cast themselves, or allow themselves to be cast, in roles that reflect aspects of their characters. In doing this they learn to see beneath superficial appearances.

study hint >>

Watch out for the possible symbolic meaning of objects such as the satellite dish and dead bird.

Jake	a habitual storyteller and natural target for bullies
Polly	quietly wise and comfortable with herself
Natasha	comes across as more confident than she really is
Carol	tries to copy Natasha but never quite hits the mark
Russell	a self-pronounced sex god!
Buzz and Speed	Russell's indistinguishable sidekicks
Shane	says little but is a mysterious presence
Finn	his huge, powerful exterior hides his real softness

>> practice questions

1   How would the actor playing Finn need to communicate his role to the audience to show that, while he may at first appear frightening, he is in fact a vulnerable character?

2   Make a list of all the things that must be on the stage at the start of the play. Draw a plan of the set and make four copies of it. Annotate one to show where different objects such as Jake's armchair, the metal steps, umbrella and pram etc. should be positioned.

3   Choose three key moments of the play. Use your remaining three set plans and mark where you would position the characters to show their relationship with each other at each moment.

4   Create a table of four columns to show which part each character plays in the story of Sparkleshark (for example, Polly plays the princess). Say how their part in the story reflects their real character. In the last column, say what they have learned by playing the part.

Stone Cold

 Stone Cold is based on Robert Swindell's award-winning novel.

Stone Cold It is a horrifying murder story which shows the brutal realities of homelessness.

Background

Every year, 43 000 young people are recorded missing. One in 20 young people are likely to experience homelessness at some time; many have been pushed out of their family homes or are running away from physical or sexual abuse. Contrary to popular belief, over 80 per cent of young homeless people have never been in trouble with the police. Most actively seek work, but with no permanent address and no income, presenting yourself well is difficult. Life on the streets can be dangerous, and young homeless people are especially vulnerable. The characters in *Stone Cold* are fictitious but the events it depicts could be real.

Plot line

David finds it impossible to live with his Mum's new boyfriend. He sets off to start a new life in London but soon finds himself living on the streets. He adopts the name Link and begins to learn some survival tactics. Meanwhile, a psychopath (Shelter) has set himself the task of cleaning up the streets by luring young homeless people into his flat where he murders them, dresses them in army uniforms, and buries them under the floorboards.

A journalist, Louise, is sent out undercover as Gail to investigate the disappearances. She meets Link. When the two of them follow up a lead, Link is lured into Shelter's flat. He finds a watch that was stolen from him and realises he is in trouble. Just as he is about to be strangled, Gail/Louise bursts in with the police. Link is saved but angry at the way Gail has deceived him.

The play ends with Shelter in prison where he is kept warm and well fed. Link returns to the street.

Main characters

Link	could be any 16-year-old
Shelter	psychopathic ex-military man
Louise/Gail	a young reporter
Joan	Link's mum; blind to what is really going on in her family
Vince	Joan's boyfriend; in order to get what he wants from her he gets rid of Link
Carol	Link's sister; she also hates Vince (he once tried it on with her) but now lives with her boyfriend, Mike
Ginger	a homeless boy; Link's friend

Major themes

The play explores some of the reasons why young people leave home and the dangers they face on the streets. Shelter is a maniac, but many of the views he expresses about young homeless people are common, so the play asks members of its audience to reconsider their attitudes and behaviour. Ultimately, the irony is that society pays to look after characters like Shelter but does little to help people like David.

study hint >>

Slideshows are used to show images of David's life. Consider how PowerPoint could be used to inform the audience about homelessness.

Stone Cold

>> practice questions

1 What would the actor playing Link need to do in order to engage the audience in Scene 1?

2 The play uses flashbacks and dream sequences to give the audience insights into David's past and hopes of a better life. Consider how you might use lights and music to signal these shifts in time to an audience.

3 Read Shelter's speech at the start of Act 1 Scene 8. What advice would you give an actor regarding how to use his voice, movement and gesture in this scene to show how dangerous and menacing Shelter is?

4 Audiences need to be 'positioned' by actors and directors in order to become emotionally engaged with the action. Look at Act 1 Scene 13. As a director, how would you try make an audience feel horrified and disgusted by the way Shelter treats Debs?

Responding to a piece of script I

- All GCSE Drama specifications require candidates to read and respond to scripts in some way.

- A script is the printed dialogue and stage directions on which a performance is based.

- A script needs to be interpreted in different ways in order for it to be performed.

Drama in time and space

Every time you open a particular play script the words will be exactly the same, just as they are in a novel or a poem. Every time you see a performance of that play though there will always be some differences. This might be to do with you. What you see and hear, and how you understand and feel about that, might be affected by:

- the mood you are in
- where you are sitting (and who with!)
- how many times you have seen or read the play before.

Or it might be to do with the performance. Perhaps the actors speak their lines a little more quickly or one has found a new way of delivering a particular line that has a particular effect. Perhaps the way they use the space or look at each other has changed slightly.

study hint >>

You need to show an understanding of what actors, directors, designers and technicians have to do to turn a script from words on a page into a performance on stage.

study hint >>

The meaning of a drama in performance is affected by time and space. The script is just the foundation on which the performance is built.

First responses

The first thing to do when you are asked to examine a piece of script is read it! Read every word, including the characters' names and all of the stage directions.

- Make a note of your initial impression.
- Is there a hint of humour, sadness or mystery about the extract?
- Does the extract give you any hint about what the play as a whole might be about?
- Try to imagine the extract being acted out. Where would the characters be in relation to each other? What would the set look like?

Read the extract through again. Annotate it with your ideas about how lines might be spoken and what sort of actions the actors might make.

study hint >>

Plays are acted out on stage. They are not real life.

Who is the playwright addressing?

In performance, an audience will hear the words spoken by actors and see them move about the set. They will also hear any sound effects and see visual effects.

A script may give a number of different people instructions about what must happen on stage, when it must happen and how.

Consider the way the writer of this stage direction demands the attention of a number of different specialists in order to bring it to life:

study hint >>

Characters' names can sometimes provide clues about what they are like or where they come from.

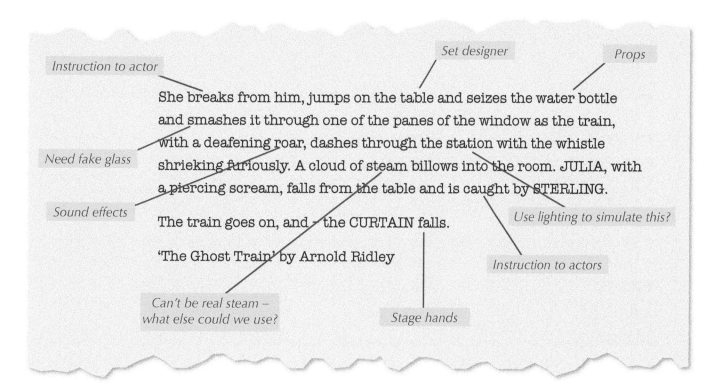

Instruction to actor · Set designer · Props

She breaks from him, jumps on the table and seizes the water bottle and smashes it through one of the panes of the window as the train, with a deafening roar, dashes through the station with the whistle shrieking furiously. A cloud of steam billows into the room. JULIA, with a piercing scream, falls from the table and is caught by STERLING.

The train goes on, and the CURTAIN falls.

'The Ghost Train' by Arnold Ridley

Need fake glass · Sound effects · Use lighting to simulate this? · Instruction to actors · Can't be real steam – what else could we use? · Stage hands

Responding to a piece of script II

Inspecting the dialogue

When faced with a new script all you have to go on is the language.
You need to consider what clues this gives you about:

- when the play is set
- where it is set
- what genre it seems to be
- what the characters are like
- what they feel about the situation they are in
- what they think about each other

Dig beneath the surface. Do not take everything at face value. It may be that there is a subtext at work:

- When a character says something, do they really mean it? Is there evidence to suggest that they may be joking or hiding the truth?

Watch out for moments of irony.

- Are there moments when the characters are surprised? How is humour or pathos being created?

>> **key fact** **The dialogue of the play may seem very 'real' but it has been specially crafted to carry meaning and create dramatic effect.**

study hint >>

It is better to speculate on what seems to be the case rather than state something as fact.

>> practice questions

Read this extract carefully.

CHARLES	Nothing of a supernatural nature has happened here.
MISS BOURNE	But it might. Suppose that train should come, what should we do?
CHARLES	What train?
MISS BOURNE	Why, the ghost train that he spoke of.
CHARLES	Oh, that's just a story. *(Going back to barrier)*
MISS BOURNE	But you never know.
TEDDIE *(coming down C)*	I say, if the ghost train comes, I bags we stop it and try and get a lift.
PEGGY	Listen! *(Rising)*
CHARLES	What's up?
PEGGY	Listen! Listen

(They listen)

RICHARD — Well?

PEGGY — I could have sworn I heard a step outside.

RICHARD — A step outside?

TEDDIE *(mimicking him)* — A – step – outside.

(RICHARD goes and looks out of window)

CHARLES — This isn't like you to be jumpy, Pegs.

PEGGY — I'm absolutely certain, Charlie.

TEDDIE — We'll soon settle that. *(Opening the door and going out: then re-entering and clutching at the sides of the door. Horror-struck)*

There's – there's –

PEGGY
ELSIE } Yes? Yes?

TEDDIE *(cheerfully)* — no one about.

'The Ghost Train' by Arnold Ridley

Write annotations on this extract in response to these questions.

1   What do the names suggest about the characters and when this play is set? Are there any clues in the style of language about when the play is set?

2   What clues are there about where this scene takes place? What sort of set would you imagine being most appropriate for this scene?

3   Are there any clues about how well different characters know each other? Are there any clues about what the characters think of each other?

4   What expectations are raised at the start of this extract in terms of mood and atmosphere? How does the mood and atmosphere change by the end of the scene?

5   How does Teddie appear to be different from the other characters? What sort of voice do you imagine him having? How might he use facial expressions at different moments and to what effect?

Reviewing a live performance

🎟️ No two people will have exactly the same response to a performance. Your review should discuss what you thought and felt about it.

🎟️ Make notes on the performance after you have seen it, as soon as possible, then use these to shape your review.

Things to check

Make notes on these things before you go to the performance:

Title	What is the play called? What expectations does this set up for you?
Author	Who wrote it? Do you know anything about the writer? How does this knowledge affect your expectations?
Venue	Where is the play being performed? Does this suggest anything about how the play might be done and what sort of audience will be present?
Director/company	Do you know anything about them?
Date	When is the performance? Is this in any way significant? For example, is it the sort of play that fits with the time of year or a current news item?

Use this checklist to jot down some details about the performance:

staging   set   plot   themes   genre   costume   make-up   lighting   sound   acting

Structuring your review

The introduction of your review should state clearly:

- what play you saw
- where and when it was performed.
- who performed it
- the historical and cultural background to the play
- a brief synopsis of the plot.

Go on to discuss:

The performance of the actors

- Did the actors identify with the characters?
- How did they use voice/pauses as part of their character?
- How did they use movement, facial expressions and gesture as part of the character?
- How did they interact on stage?

The technical aspects

- What type of acting area was used? Why do you think that particular was chosen?
- What was the style of the production? Naturalistic or symbolic?
- What was the scenic design? Did it reflect the themes of the play?
- What effect was achieved with lighting and sound?
- How did costume, make-up and hair help to develop the characters?

What the play was saying

- What were the key messages of the play?
- How were they communicated to the audience?
- What did the director seem to want to achieve?
- How did the audience react?

Conclude your review by saying:

- what your personal response to the performance was
- what you particularly enjoyed about it – be as specific as possible
- what the performance meant to you
- what you didn't like so much and why.

Setting the context

Your review will benefit by making comparisons with other productions you might have seen and demonstrating that you have some knowledge of the cultural and historical context. For example: 'The two Shakespearean productions I saw were completely different. "Romeo and Juliet" was a modern interpretation set in the round. It drew on Indian theatre forms in order to highlight the relevance of the play to contemporary cultural and religious tensions. "Twelfth Night" was set in Elizabethan times and was presented on a thrust stage.'

Use subject-specific terminology and include annotated diagrams of costumes and set designs, if possible, to illustrate your point.

study hint >>

Always make reference to a specific scene to illustrate the point (e.g. 'At the start of the play, Mr Craven entered dressed in a black suit. This symbolised that he was in mourning after his wife had died. The colour of his clothes also showed he was a very serious character.').

Devising drama

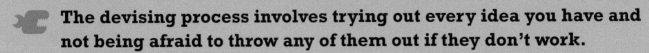
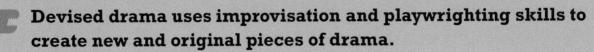
Responding to a stimulus

Anything can be used as a stimulus for a devised drama. You may be given a poem, a picture, a newspaper article or an object to work with or you may have the opportunity to work on an idea of your own. Be playful and try to look at things from different angles. For example, if you are given a photograph of an incident:

- look at what the people in the background are doing and consider the incident from their point of view

- if inanimate objects such as trees, lamp posts or pieces of furniture could talk, imagine how they might report the incident

- if the incident was witnessed by an alien, how would they interpret what was happening?

Getting started

There is no one right way to launch the devising process. The key thing is to try out ideas in action rather than just talk about them. Try the following:

- Start with a place: an office, a classroom, a spaceship, the gates of heaven, the pit of hell. Experiment with ways of establishing a sense of place physically and vocally.

- Start with a discovery: a dead body is found; a threatening text message appears on a mobile phone; a person feels a lump on their body. How do people react to the discovery? Perhaps the drama will come from people not reacting as you might normally expect.

- Start with a tense situation: a lift that jams between floors; an explosion throws an underground train into darkness; a man condemned to death sits in his cell.

- Start with the arrival of a new character: someone turns up in a situation and stirs up some trouble. How does their arrival change people's attitudes and behaviour?

- Start with a simple line of dialogue: 'I'm really not feeling too well, you know.' 'Stay calm, but whatever you do, just don't turn round!'

Accepting and blocking

Improvising on your feet will generate more ideas than sitting around discussing what you might do. The best ideas are often those produced spontaneously. Agree on a starting point, and see what happens. For example:

'Two people sit in an attic room. Someone walks in and…'
'A dead body lies on the ground. Into the scene walks…'
'It is the night before the execution. The condemned man turns to his guard and says…'

Improvisations die if one of the players blocks an idea:
'Your secretary called me about Sarah. I came as quickly as I could.'
'I haven't got a secretary. Who's Sarah?'

Try to accept what is offered and move it on:
'Your secretary called me about Sarah. I came as quickly as I could.'
'Thank you. It's not good news, I'm afraid. Tell me, has anything like this ever happened to Sarah before?'

Sometimes blocking can help to move an improvisation into a new direction if it also accepts the situation:
'Your secretary called me about Sarah. I came as quickly as I could.'
'No Sarah here. Are you sure you're in the right place?'
'It's my daughter, Sarah. I was told she'd had an accident. Isn't this the hospital?'
'No sir, this is a garage but we do repairs if that's any help.'

study hint >>

Don't drop ideas too quickly. Be patient. Keep trying out new ways of approaching the stimulus rather than choosing a new one.

study hint >>

Make sure you document the process of devising and evaluate the final outcome.

Structuring the drama

Identify a key moment and work backwards and forwards from that. For example, if you are given the title 'Protest' as a starting point, make a still image of a protest taking place. Make a second image to show what sparked the protest. Add a third image to show the consequence of the protest. In this way, you can create a three-frame story, which can be recorded like a cartoon showing stick men:

The first frame shows one stick man being beaten by a soldier.

The second frame shows group of stick men waving banners.

The third frame shows soldiers confronting protesters with guns.

Give each frame a caption. Try writing a description of what is happening in the scene by using this caption as an acrostic.

If the characters shown in each frame could speak one line what would they say?

If each character could think aloud one thing, what would that be?

If each character could comment on the incident from their perspective, how could *direct address* be used to communicate this to an audience?

Moving to a performance

Improvise around the narrative as it develops. Try using physical theatre or other non-naturalistic techniques to represent scenes and characters. Make a note of every idea you have and how you tried it out.

Select which ideas you want to keep and develop further, and decide on a possible running order.

Rehearse the play as you would if you were working on a script but always stay open to new ideas and techniques to keep the drama feeling fresh.

Evaluating devised drama

- You need to be able to critically analyse what you and other members of your group did in the process of creating and performing your own drama.

- Use subject-specific terminology and try to relate what you did to other drama you have seen.

Putting the play into context

State who you were working with and why you chose to work with them. Describe briefly what your devised drama was about and what influenced your decision to choose that particular idea. Try and give some background to your ideas. For example:

Our play explored a tragedy that occurred in 2004 when 21 migrant Chinese workers were drowned in Morecombe Bay where they were picking cockles. Having been inspired by a drama lesson based on the story, we researched the incident further. We were moved by some of the personal stories we discovered but also shocked to learn about the way the workers had been treated and how hard their lives were. We thought that dramatising such a serious and sensitive story would be challenging but give us the opportunity to use a number of non-naturalistic techniques.

Messages and themes

Discuss the messages, themes and dramatic issues that your group wanted to convey to the audience. You should make reference to specific parts of your play and analysis how you tried to make the message clear through your drama.

An important theme in our play was exploitation and how hard the workers had to work for so little pay. They got just £5 for every 25 kg bag of cockles. We tried to show this at the start of the play by standing in a semicircle and playing a game of catch. First we threw a ping-pong ball to each other, then swopped it for a tennis ball, football, medicine ball and finally a sack of potatoes. Every time someone threw the ball or sack they'd say 'think of the money'. As the game went on the actors showed they were getting more and more tired. Finally, they picked up the sack together and gave it to The Boss who then slowly peeled a £5 note from a wodge of notes and held it in front of them as the lights dimmed.

The rehearsal process

Describe how the play developed through the rehearsal process. Think about the decisions you made as a group and analyse the effect these had on the final piece. For example:

At first we tried to use Chinese accents but quickly realised this sounded insulting and comical. We wanted to suggest that communicating in English was difficult for some of the characters. Our solution was to have the characters of the workers speak slowly and carefully when they were talking to The Boss and other English characters but talk faster and use more gestures when they were speaking amongst themselves.

Mention the techniques you used in the devising process that gave you a deeper insight into your character and the theme of your drama, for example, hot-seating, role-on-the-wall, centring.

Technical aspects

Outline the technical aspects of your drama and discuss the contribution they made to the overall dramatic effectiveness of the work.

- Set design – was your set naturalistic or minimalist? What kind of environment did you want to create? What problems did you encounter with the set? What worked well? Where did you position objects? Was it successful in the final performance?

- Props – were they symbolic? Were they necessary in the development of the plot? What did the audience learn about a character from individual props?

- Lighting – how was lighting used to create mood, atmosphere, location and so on?

- Music and sound effects – why was a particular piece of music used? Where was it used and what effect did it create?

- Costume, hair and make-up – did your costume show the period in which your play was set? What garments did you wear? What colour and fabric did you choose? What did we learn about character and the style of the play from your costume choice?

> **study hint >>**
>
> **Include visual evidence in your evaluation e.g. set and costume designs, diagrams, photographs. Give each illustration a caption or annotate it to make it clear what you are illustrating and why.**

Evaluating the final performance

Avoid saying things such as, 'I was very nervous but it went well and I didn't forget my lines.' Break your evaluation down into sections:

Your performance	Discuss your use of voice and movement, how you used space, how you handled props. What scenes did you perform well and why? Where could you have improved? How did the audience respond to your character?
The group performance	Which scenes were effective from a group point of view? How did the group co-operate, pick up cues and so on.
Technical elements	How successful were the lighting and sound effects? Was the performance space used effectively?
The audience response	How did the audience respond to particular moments? What was the overall atmosphere like for them? What did you learn from this experience and how will it help you in future devised projects?

>> practice questions

1. Analyse and evaluate your group's devised performance. Include details of how members of the group developed their performances and what the audience's response was to them.

2. Discuss the different theatrical techniques and style your group chose to use in your devised performance. Explain why you made these choices and what contribution they had to the overall dramatic effectiveness of the performance.

3. Discuss how other performances you have seen, or dramas you have been involved in, influenced your devised performance.

From page to stage

- Identify what you think the author is trying to say in the play. What are their intentions?

- Keep reminding yourself of what the play means to you as you work on bringing the script to life.

Choosing a script

A script must interest you – if it does this, you will feel more keen to work out the problems involved in staging it. Don't grab at the first play that turns up or choose one just because it has the right number of parts. Reading a copy of the whole play, or better still seeing it, will help you enormously. Everyone in the group should read the script before agreeing to perform it. Read it through as a group at least three times. Swop parts each time in order to get a feel for which characters suit which actors best. Make sure you all understand:

- where and when the play is set
- what the mood and atmosphere are like
- what actually happens
- what sort of people the characters are.

Getting started

Have a plan. Decide:

- who's going to watch the play
- where it will be staged
- how long the piece will be
- what technical support you will need
- how long you have to prepare.

Draw up a timetable of what you think needs to happen by certain times and try to stick to the deadlines you have set yourselves.

> **study hint >>**
>
> **You can't stage a play by talking about it! Get into action as soon as possible to try out your ideas.**

Get into action

'Walk' through the play by setting up an area which is roughly where you'd imagine the play to be set. Use chairs or tape marks on the floor to provide an outline. If moving around the marked-out area seems difficult, try to act out the scene by having someone else read the lines while you provide the actions. Without the book to distract you, you will be able to concentrate more on your movements and facial expressions.

Improvise the play using your own words so that you can identify the key bits of action and get a sense of what the characters are like. Using one or two props or pieces of costume can help an actor get into character. Some costumes and or a mask can present big problems to an actor if he or she is not used to it, in which case you should rehearse with them as much as possible.

Putting down the script

Start learning your lines straight away. The sooner you can put down the script, the sooner you will be able to start building your character by using your hands and facial expressions.

What sort of learner are you?

- Aural learning: record your lines electronically and speak along with them when they are played back.

- Visual learning: highlighting lines in different colours works well for some people. Try sticking your lines onto the bathroom wall so they can be read while you are on the loo!

- Verbal learning: work with another person who will read all of the lines of the other characters so that your lines are always spoken in the context of the script as a whole.

- Kinaesthetic learning: physically write your lines out. Read them through out loud and put a movement to each line.

Final preparation

Have a technical rehearsal to make sure that all of the cues for lighting and sound effects are in the right place and you have all the props you need.

Follow this with a full dress rehearsal. Treat the dress rehearsal as a performance (it's useful to invite a friendly audience who can give you feedback).

study hint >>

Document and evaluate your work. Keeping a working notebook or rehearsal log of your preparations is essential.

>> practice questions

1 Use examples from the text to explain how you used voice, movement, gesture and facial expression to communicate the role of your chosen character to an audience.

2 Explain how your group communicated mood and atmosphere to an audience through both their performances and the technical and design elements you used.

Documenting your work I

- Recording your ideas and what you have seen, read and done in a journal or working notebook will help you analyse and evaluate the way your drama skills and understanding develops.

- Update your documentation regularly rather than trying to remember what you did months after doing it.

Recording first responses

Whether you are working on a published play script, creating a piece of devised drama from a given stimulus, or exploring a theme or dramatic genre in a workshop, you should record your initial responses. Say what you first thought and felt about what you are working with. Try to relate it to other things you have seen and done.

- Give a brief description of the text you have set out to explore.

- State which explorative strategies you used to develop your understanding of the text.

- Say why you chose these strategies and how they helped to develop your understanding.

A drama text is anything that might be used as a starting point for dramatic exploration. The text might be:

- a poem

- an object

- a piece of music

- an extract from a play script

- a piece of live theatre

- an extract from a film or television programme

- a newspaper or magazine article

- an extract from a novel or piece of non-fiction.

Make brief notes on which explorative strategies you used to explore the text, why you used them and what the result was.

Explorative strategy	Why did we use it?	What did we find out?
still image		
thought tracking		
narrating		
hot-seating		
role play		
cross-cutting		
forum theatre		
marking the moment		

Annotated photographs can be used very effectively to show you and your group at work. Using a digital camera will allow you to alter the size of the images to suit your presentation and perhaps even add speech balloons and thought bubbles to the images electronically.

Developing your ideas

You need to document:

- how your exploration of the drama text developed through the use of the drama medium and the elements of drama
- how a script or devised drama has emerged from your work on the drama text
- how your understanding and interpretation of the themes and issues arising from the text have developed.

The drama medium involves the purposeful use of the following to communicate meaning to an audience:

- costume, masks and make-up
- sound effects and music
- lighting
- space and levels
- set and props
- movement, mime and gesture
- voice
- spoken language

Make brief notes on which elements of drama you focused on when developing your drama, how and why.

Element of drama	How and why did we focus on this?
action, plot and content	
forms	
climax and anticlimax	
rhythm, pace and tempo	
contrasts	
characterisation	
conventions	
symbols	

Documenting your work II

Perhaps the most important part of your documentation will be the section in which you analyse and reflect on what you have created and learned through your practical work. As well as critically evaluating your own contributions and performance, you should say what other people in your group achieved. You should show a knowledge and understanding of the social, cultural and historical context of the drama texts or play you have been working on and how this has influenced your work. As far as possible, you should mention how other performances you have seen have contributed to your understanding of drama and the development of your own skills and ideas.

Make brief notes to help you evaluate:

Self-evaluation	What contribution did you make?	
	What special responsibilities did you have?	
	How well do you think you performed your tasks?	
	What was the most satisfying part of the project for you?	
	Were you disappointed with yourself for some reason?	
	What did you learn about yourself?	
	What else did you learn?	
Group evaluation	How well did other members of your group do in the project?	
	What impressed you in particular about their contribution?	
	How well did you work as a team?	
	Were there difficulties working together? How did you overcome them?	
	What did you learn about each other?	
Context	How does your work relate to other dramas you have seen or read?	
	How has your work been influenced by your study of the historical, social and cultural context of drama?	

Presenting your coursework

If you are required to submit documentary evidence of your course as a part of your final assessment your submission should reflect your understanding that drama is a *visual* and *enactive* art form.

Successful portfolios have a good content, which explains and demonstrates a candidate's knowledge, understanding and creativity. They are also:

- attractively laid out
- accurately written
- interesting to read and look at.

You might use sheets of A3 paper or card to set out your documentation as a series of posters containing:

- annotated photographs and sketches
- annotated extracts of scripts
- storyboards
- designs (these can be done on sheets of acetate which are overlain one upon the other to show the design at different stages)
- swatches of fabric
- examples of sound or lighting cues sheets.

The written content of your documentation may be handwritten or word-processed. You may use a computer to assist in the design.

> **study hint >>**
>
> Your teacher can advise you on the way you present your documentation, but they must be able to state that you have done the work yourself.

Evaluating a live production

Preparing your evaluation

Make brief notes to remind yourself which dramatic techniques were used in the production, for example:

> narration   song   chorus   physical   theatre   mime

Make notes on the most *significant moments* in the production. Why were these moments significant? Were they, for example:

- a turning point in the story
- a moment of tension or surprise
- a sad or comic moment
- a moment that communicated character
- a moment that communicated relationships between characters
- a visually striking moment?

Discussing performance

Discuss in detail what you felt to be **either** the strongest **or** the weakest performance by **one** actor and explain the reasons for the strengths or weaknesses. You will need to give details of a particular scene or section.

Discuss the actor's:

- use of voice
- use of body movement, posture, gesture
- use of face
- interaction with others.

In what specific moments in the selected scene or section did the actor impress or disappoint you and why? What was the reaction of the rest of the audience?

Discussing technical aspects

Choose a production you have seen during your course in which the design or technical aspects surprised you. Discuss in detail how either the design or technical aspects contributed to the overall effectiveness of one section of the production and explain in what ways you found it surprising.

Consider:

- style of production
- communication of period and place
- fabrics, textures, colours
- use of space and levels
- use of sound
- use of lighting
- use of management and properties
- use of make-up
- use of masks
- visual impact
- audience reaction.

Use sketches and diagrams to illustrate your points.

study hint >>

Sketches and diagrams need to be a decent size so the examiner can see what they are showing. Add annotations to emphasise the important points of what you are trying to show. Putting little drawings down in the corner of the page with no explanation of what they are doing there will be a waste of your time.

Discussing the overall impact

Choose a production you have seen during your course that created a strong audience response. Discuss in detail the scene or section that made the strongest impression and explain how the effect on the audience was created.

Make sure that:

- your response is a personal evaluation of what you have seen
- you use specific examples from the play to illustrate your points.

Where relevant, discuss:

- style of production
- communication of period and place
- use of space and levels
- quality of movement
- interaction between characters
- costumes: fabrics, textures, colours
- use of make-up, masks and puppets
- lighting and sound
- audience reaction
- visual and emotional impact.

War Horse

Question

Choose one play that you have studied during your course. Select one extract from the play. Discuss how you would communicate one of the main characters to an audience through your use of voice, movement, gesture and facial expression. Give clear examples from the play to support your answer.

>> Answer

In Act 1 of 'Billy Liar' by Keith Waterhouse, edition XX, from 'ALICE goes out into the hall and puts on a coat which is hanging on the rack... ' to 'FLORENCE crosses the room and disappears up the stairs into the bedroom' the role of Billy is a key one.[1] The start of this scene is basically Geoffrey telling Billy off, yet it would have to be shown that Billy wasn't particularly bothered. This can be achieved by the actor standing with his hands in his pockets, slumping maybe. Eye contact with Geoffrey would be minimal to show that he wasn't really listening. Billy could also gaze around or fidget with his hands. Occasionally nodding his head in acknowledgement of what his father was saying.[2]

As Billy walks into the kitchen, I feel he should have a slow and shuffling walk, as if he has just woken up, and is in no hurry to get to anywhere. Once Alice and Geoffrey leave and Billy is left alone with his grandmother, Florence, I feel that there should be far more silences, with Billy's eyes wandering, as if looking for something to do. 'I can't eat that egg. It's stone cold.' This should be said with a slightly whinging and disappointed tone, to display the fact that Billy is slightly immature. Yet when Florence starts her speech on how 'There's too much waste in this house... ' the actor playing Billy should sink back into his chair, possibly roll his eyes and give sarcastic nods and smiles at intervals and a long sigh from him when she finishes.[3]

'BILLY drinks and grimaces'. Here the actor should look, not at Florence, but maybe at his own cup of tea, possibly searching for a new conversation to bring up as opposed to sitting and listening to Florence's views on food waste.

A terribly important part of the scene is where both characters begin to go off into their own dream worlds.[4] At this stage it must be shown that Billy is starting to drift off as he says 'Sitting in a coffee bar... ' the actor would possibly begin to gaze, with eyes slowly glazing over as the character sinks deeper into his fantasy. Where the full stops are in his sentences, there must be rather long pauses in speech, to show him contemplating which direction the day dream will go in. 'Espresso with a girl. Duffel coat and dirty toenails.'

The actor could possibly put his arm around Florence, showing Billy is so deeply engrossed in his fantasy that he sees his grandmother as the imaginary girl. Yet whilst Florence is still wittering on about life when she was young, Billy's face would still be facing forwards, still gazing, maybe pretending to listen to the troubles of the suicidal girl. 'I discovered her the night before, contemplating suicide.' Billy would now be sat upright in his chair, and leaning forwards to get closer to this imaginary girl. He could nod and give empathetic smiles as he tries to comfort her, 'less than a week ago my father felt the same as you.'

Suicidal.' His tone of voice would be gentle and slightly regretful, with a slight, small, 'brave' smile on his face.[5]

'Well, he'll never be world champion now. A broken man on two tin legs.'[6] Billy should now stand up, shaking his head at the tragic nature of his day dream, looking at the ground, and then start to limp, groaning and leaning against furniture with an anguished look on his face, biting his lip at trying to ignore his imaginary pain. Then as Florence says 'He's not right in the head.' Billy should suddenly become sheepish as he knows he is being watched. Standing up straight, no longer leaning on the furniture, and then start to rub his leg. As he offers the explanation of 'cramp', his eyes would be on his legs, refusing to meet Florence's stare.[7]

A slight expression of relief should spread across Billy's face as the doorbell goes, as it offers him a release from the awkward situation building with Florence, and so he should rush to answer it. As Arthur and Billy do their 'routine' it should all be terribly over-acted, with large gestures, such as Billy stamping his foot firmly on the ground and making a slight punching gesture in the air as he says 'They'll stand for him and lump it'. As he says 'Into the house Ned and bar the door!' he should almost shout and point wildly into his own house with a look of mock urgency on his face.[8]

The actor should double over clutching his stomach as the pair 'dissolve into laughter'. As they return inside, Billy should completely ignore the random comments made by Florence. He should once again be relaxed with a shuffling lazy walk going slowly back into the kitchen to finish his tea. 'Isn't it my Saturday off?' said with confusion and a furrowed brow as he sips his tea, slowly. Possibly with a slight guilty expression as well, to see his friend angry at him. His voice would be smaller and weaker than before, where he displayed such non-caring and idiocy.

As Florence gets up to leave, Billy could risk a cheeky sticking out of the tongue at her behind her back before turning once again to face Arthur at the end of the scene section.

>> Commentary on the answer

1 Specifies play and edition.

2 Explains what Billy is feeling – 'not bothered' – and how the actor can show this.

3 Explains how the actor could move and use his voice and gives specific references to the text.

4 Recognises that at this point in the scene a change in mood occurs and this must be reflected in the actions.

5 A good example of referencing voice and movement and relationship with other characters.

6 Recognises the point at which the tension changes as humour is injected and shows how the actor can interpret this.

7 Illustrates the relationship to another character.

8 Again, an example of physical interpretation of the text.

   A sound discussion with detailed justification of how the role of Billy can be realised on stage.

Question

Choose a production you have seen during your course that you considered successful.

Discuss, in detail, the contribution of one performer to the success of the production. You will need to give details of at least one particular scene or section and include reference to voice, movement, characterisation and relationships between characters on stage.

>> Answer

I thought the musical 'Blood Brothers' by Willie Russell was successful. I saw it at the Adelphi Theatre in London. The character who I thought added specifically to this success was Mickey.[1] This was because as the character changed and grew, so did the actor and his behaviour, which portrayed the character very well.[2]

Firstly the actor playing Mickey was a full-grown man, and so he had to exaggerate and emphasise his actions a lot, to give the audience the impression of a child. He used a high-pitched voice and spoke very fast and excitedly. The character is very outlandish and energetic, so the actor used most of the stage space, by making his movements large and 'over the top'.[3] For instance, when Mickey is pretending to drive a car, the actor jumped onto the floor, and thrust his arms and legs out in front of him, as though he were gripping a steering wheel. As he veers left and right the actor leans violently all the way over to one side or another. He makes loud car noises that differ according to his actions, and as he 'stops' he screeches loudly, leans all the way back, springs up, and bumps across the stage. His eyes are wide and he smiles with his teeth biting his lower lip to show his excitement.[4]

Another example of the actor portraying a child well is when Mickey pretends to ride a horse. The actor really does act as though he believed that there was an invisible horse. When mounting or dismounting it the actor swings his leg round in the air, he 'ties it up', pretends to pat and stroke it, and 'talks' to it, just as a child would if he was playing. He gallops around the stage making horse noises and imitates pulling the reins tightly to stop it. The audience find this effective because the actor is apparently playing, and illustrating the kind of innocent games that children play to express their vivid imaginations.[5]

The actor's interaction with Eddie is also very realistic.[6] Mickey wants to impress Eddie so he starts being naughty to show off. When the actor playing Mickey pretends to spit he leans really far back and then throws himself forward, as if he were making a tremendous effort. Afterwards, he sways back and forth on his heels beaming and looking really pleased with himself.

As the play progresses, so do the characters, and as they age time-wise, so the actors have to, visually, for the audience. Mickey reaches puberty, and as a teenager he has hit an awkward stage in his life.[7] The actor spends no time on the floor now, his stature changes to show an increase in maturity. When Mickey boasts to Eddie, the actor puffs out his chest and talks boldly in a loud, confident voice, but as soon as Linda comes along, he stops in his tracks. His stature shrinks a little, he stuffs his hands in his pockets and bows his head. Because he becomes worried about embarrassment, the actor pauses before talking to Linda, he makes no eye contact and stares at the ground instead and scuffs his feet so as to detract from what he's saying. He appears more nervous and less forward. The audience think this is funny and sympathises with him because many of them have experienced this themselves. When Mickey finishes talking to Linda the actor runs away laughing with Eddie to mask his embarrassment.

Again the play moves on. Mickey has just got out of prison and his attitude completely changes; the character becomes someone else. His stature reverts back down because the actor slumps his shoulders, he leans on walls for support because the actor has become weak. His speech becomes slow and minimal, his expression is constantly angry and dark, he screws up his face and constantly stares at the floor, his expression doesn't ever relax or change, he shuffles rather than walks and he looks completely dull and lifeless. He no longer raises his head to talk to anyone and makes no eye contact. This makes him seem cold and heartless and the audience's opinion of him completely changes. The actor appears to be unfriendly and aggressive. He occasionally loses his temper and explodes in a fury, he goes red, begins to shout and throw his arms into the air, and he remains in one place, but this stops abruptly and he sinks back into the shell of an empty, walking man. He seems miserable and spaced out, his eyes don't seem to move and the audience feels sorry for him because his life seems so hopeless, but the actor also makes the audience feel dislike as well now for the character because he shuts his family out and treats them so badly.[8]

This is why I feel that the actor playing Mickey was so effective in making the production successful, because he made it so plainly obvious to the audience how the character felt, there was visual evidence that one can comprehend and relate to which made the perception and understanding of the play all the easier.

>> Commentary on the answer

1   States that the production was successful and identifies the chosen character thus answering the question.

2   Distinguishes between actor and character.

3   Refers to vocal and movement skills and the impression they create.

4   Gives an example of what the actor did on stage.

5   Gives an example of the actor's movements and references the audience response.

6   Reference to a specific moment.

7   Refers to the actor's physical movements and use of voice and their relevance to the plot as time passes.

8   Explains how the actor interprets his changed circumstances through his movement and speech and the effect these have on the audience.

This is a sound and competent discussion with constant reference to audience response and specific moments.

study hint >>

Don't just describe – analyse.

Specimen answer on a live production: technical

Choose a production you have seen during your course in which you felt design helped to create a strong effect on you as a member of the audience.

Discuss, in detail, at least one scene or section in which the design elements had a strong effect on you.

>> Answer

I found 'The Woman in Black' by Stephen Mallatrat adapted from the novel by Susan Hill, which I saw at The Fortune Theatre in London, to be a very frightening play.[1] As there are only two actors it needs a lot of design to keep the production not only interesting but also effective.[2]

In one section, 'The Actor' playing the character of Arthur Kipps is visiting the house of a lady who died, in order to take care of her possessions. Apart from a dog he is completely alone in the house. After a long day sorting through the lady's papers he tries to go to sleep, but he is laying down for about 20 to 30 seconds when he hears the sound of what seems to be a heartbeat. Arthur Kipps wakes up and the noise stops, but when he lies down it starts again. He goes to investigate and comes to a door that had never been opened before. As he approaches the door the noise becomes louder. Suddenly, we hear a blood-curdling scream, the 'heartbeat' stops abruptly and the lights go out. A gauze is used in the production and, as the lights come up behind the gauze we see that there is a bedroom behind it. We can now see that the noise was not a heartbeat but the sound of a rocking chair moving with no-one in it. I found this particular section very effective and successful. It required very accurate timing to create the correct effect.[3]

The gauze is a very effective part of the staging as it allows the scene to be changed without the audience being aware. In the previous scene the area behind the gauze represented a graveyard and the gauze gave it a foggy and very eerie effect.

When the gauze is lit from behind the audience can see the area of stage behind, but if it is only lit from the front then the audience cannot see behind it. This allows the action to continue while the scene behind the gauze is changed and this can be used very effectively. In this production the gauze was also used as a screen for projections. In the church scene of the funeral of Mrs Drablow a large crucifix was projected onto the screen and whenever 'The Actor' or Arthur Kipps approached Eel March House a projection of the house appeared on the gauze.[4]

The production used only a minimum of props and costumes. Sometimes only a jacket and a hat were used to distinguish two characters. Other props were made to represent several things. A wicker basket was used as the pony and trap, the seat on the train, a desk and a bed. There was a clothes rail stage right that allowed the actors to change easily between their characters without having to leave the stage.[5]

Sound effects were used effectively throughout the performance to build the scenes. Crows cawed in the background at the funeral scene, there was a howling wind on the foggy night and seagulls were heard outside when they were near Eel Marsh House as it was near the sea.[6] The music box which was used in Act 2 was very eerie. When Arthur Kipps first went into the child's bedroom he played with the music box but later on, we heard a scream and the stage went completely black. The audience was silent, and then we heard the sound of a music box and Arthur Kipps re-entered the room to find it trashed and the rocking chair moving by itself.[7]

Overall I think that the lighting, sound effects, minimal props and costumes made 'The Woman in Black' very effective. The timing of light and sound was perfect and evoked the full response from the audience. I saw the play a second time at the New Victoria Theatre in Woking but it did not have the same effect on me because I knew when certain 'frightening' things were about to happen.[8]

>> Commentary on the answer

1   States where the production was seen.

2   Provides the context for the need for 'a lot of design'.

3   A vivid description of the 'heartbeat' scene in Eel Marsh House. Good awareness of the need for timing but this point could be developed more.

4   Addresses the way in which the gauze is used and how it allows the scene to be changed without the audience knowing. Explains how the gauze works with lighting.

5   Mentions the minimal props and costumes but you could consider developing the reason why these are used – that this is a lawyer seeking the assistance of an actor to tell his story, using the facilities at hand in a closed theatre.

6   Mentions the use of sound effects but you could mention how they were used and what effect they created for the audience.

7   Good reference to the music box but the point could be developed – why was the music box so eerie? What feelings did it evoke and why?

8   A reasonably neat summary but more precision on the effects created would have improved the answer. The reference to seeing the production again is interesting but it could be developed into a useful point about the effects of surprise and the creation of tension.

Quick quizzes

The origins of theatre

1   A _____ explores themes of death, power and justice.

2   Saying that someone is a 'Thespian' means that they are an _____.

3   _____ was a well-known writer of Roman comedies.

4   Mystery plays were staged on moveable _____ _____ .

5   Commedia dell'arte troupes developed ideas for different scenes from brief descriptions of the action called _____ .

The theatre explosion

1   'The Theatre' was built in London in 1576 by _____ _____ .

2   Queen _____ was on the thrown when Shakespeare started writing his plays.

3   The first women actors appeared on stage in England during the reign of

    _____ ____ .

4   Melodrama was a popular form of entertainment in _____ Britain.

5   Melodramas relied on fast action and _____ to entertain the audience.

Theatre in the modern world

1   Naturalism attempted to show _____ _____ on stage.

2   Bertolt Brecht was a _____ from _____ .

3   'The Method' was a system of acting that was built on some of the ideas of the Russian director

    _____ _____ .

4   Samuel Beckett's plays are sometimes regarded as examples of the _____ of

    the _____ .

5   Some of the new British writers of the 1950s were referred to as the

    _____ _____ _____ .

The origins of theatre
1 tragedy 2 actor 3 Plautus 4 pageant wagons 5 scenario

The theatre explosion
1 James Burbage 2 Elizabeth I 3 Charles II 4 Victorian 5 sentimentality

Theatre in the modern world
1 real life 2 playwright, Germany 3 Konstantin Stanislavski 4 Theatre of the absurd 5 Angry Young Men

The language of drama

Match the key term to the definition in the boxes on the following page,
e.g. 1 tableau = 7 A group of actors standing in a still image.

The answers are at the bottom of p 85.

Key term		Definition	
1	tableau	1	sound effects
2	thought-tracking	2	a type of drama in which the characters are played as if they were real people in a real world
3	narration	3	the 'type' or family that a drama belongs to
4	cyclorama	4	a line made up by an actor which isn't in the script
5	forum theatre	5	the part taken by an actor
6	plot	6	the term used when something is going on beneath what the characters are actually saying
7	FX	7	a group of actors standing in a still image
8	climax	8	the movement made by an actor which has a particular meaning
9	ensemble	9	a technique used by actors to build a character by thinking of one part of their body
10	genre	10	a form of theatre in which the audience is actively involved in shaping or reshaping a scene
11	style	11	the lines spoken by a number of different characters to each other
12	ad-lib	12	the term for a group of actors who work closely together
13	characterisation	13	the unfolding events of a story

Key term			Definition	
14	monologue	14		the moment of greatest tension
15	dialogue	15		the word used for when something stands for something else
16	melodrama	16		when a character speaks aloud what they are thinking at a given moment
17	centring	17		a remark made by a character directly to the audience
18	naturalism	18		the particular way in which something is done
19	symbol	19		a technique for telling a part of a story to the audience directly
20	sub-text	20		the way an actor uses voice, movement and gesture to show what they are like in a role
21	gesture	21		a speech made by just one character
22	aside	22		the back wall of the stage
23	proxemics	23		the word for objects used on stage
24	role	24		a term describing the way space is used to create meaning
25	props	25		a genre often associated with 'over-acting' by the characters

Key term	1	2	3	4	5	6	7	8	9	10	11	12	13
Definition	7												

Key term	14	15	16	17	18	19	20	21	22	23	24	25
Definition												

Check your knowledge of different types of stage lanterns by filling in the chart below. Write in the name of each lantern and briefly describe what it is like and what it does.

Symbol	Name	Description

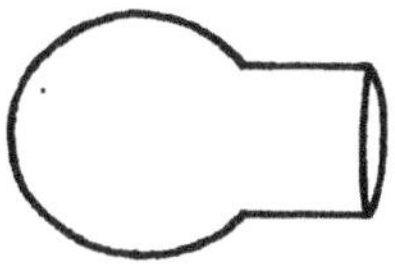

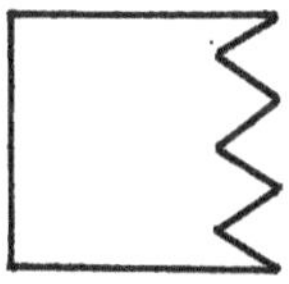

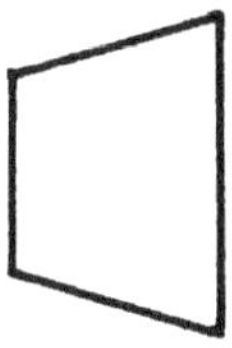

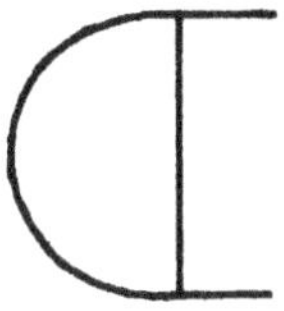

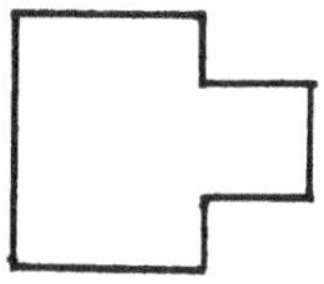

Common mistakes

You may gain a few valuable extra marks by ensuring that you:

- use subject-specific vocabulary
- know what specialist terms mean
- spell them accurately.

Common spelling mistakes include:

amphitheatre (sometimes misspelled as 'amfitheatre')
centring (sometimes misspelled as 'centering')
character
chorus (sometimes misspelled as 'choros')
narration
proscenium
proxemics
rehearsal
scene (often misspelled as 'sence')
scenery (often misspelled as 'scenary')
soliloquy
tableau (singular) tableaux (plural – note it has an '**x**', not an '**s**')
theatre (you might get away with the American spelling – 'theater' – but it is not ideal.)

Punctuation

Drama is a different subject from English but uses the same language – and the same rules! Sentences should start with capital letters and finish with full stops. Quotations should be set apart from your comments by using quotation marks.

>> **key fact** The convention is to use capital letters for names of plays and playwrights. The name of the play should be put in quotation marks. For example:
'A View From the Bridge' by Arthur Miller, 'Blue Remembered Hills' by Dennis Potter.

Dos and don'ts

Do:

- read the question carefully.
- make sure you know what you are being asked to do.
- plan your answer before you start writing.
- divide your answer into paragraphs. Put all your ideas about the same aspect into one paragraph.
- use the PQD (point, quote, develop) formula as far as possible.

  Make your **point**.

  Support what you are saying with a **quotation**.

  Develop your point further, paying attention to how things might be done.
- use annotated diagrams and sketches if they will help make your point clearer and refer to them in your written answer.
- analyse and justify.

Don't:

- waffle.
- imagine the examiner knows nothing about the play (so don't waste time re-telling the story in detail).
- imagine the examiner has exactly the same ideas about the play as you do (so don't forget to explain why you think what you do).
- use quotations without adding a comment about what they show.
- draw tiny diagrams and sketches and forget to explain what they are showing.
- make emotional judgements ('I thought it was great!') without explaining how you came to feel the way you do.

>> **key fact** Questions will be about what plays might look and sound like when they are performed.

Content and form

>> **key fact** Your discussions of drama should contain comments on both content and form and recognise that they are dependent on each other.

Content
This refers to **what** is being said in the drama.

Make sure you recognise the difference between **narrative** and **thematic content**:

'The Crucible' tells the story of a group of villagers in seventeenth century America who are accused of witchcraft. It focuses in particular on the character of John Proctor who stands by his innocence but is nevertheless hanged at the end. The play explores the themes of honesty and justice and is critical about the way governments can misuse their power.

Form
This refers to **how** it is being said. In drama things are 'said' not just through words but also through action, sound, light and design. You need to show an understanding of how the different **elements of drama** can be used to **convey meaning**:

At the end of 'The Crucible' Proctor's wife Elizabeth must look physically drained by the emotion, holding herself up by gripping the bars of the cell window. Even so, her voice could be full of pride. When she says, 'He has his goodness now. God forbid I take it from him!' the words could be delivered quite slowly and evenly and Elizabeth could make an obvious effort to hold her head up to show that she is still strong and calm inside.

As she speaks her last line a drum roll begins and builds to a threatening crescendo. It is violent and militaristic but, by contrast, the orange glow of the morning sun begins to light Elizabeth's face suggesting that she will be saved. Meanwhile the actor playing Hale should fall to his knees looking terrified and lost as he 'weeps in frantic prayer' suggesting that he knows he has done wrong and will suffer for it.

study hint >>

Drama is an art form. It tries to understand the world by looking at it in new ways. There is never just one right answer, so trust your creative ideas about how a play might be staged and what it might mean will be valued.

Sixty key words

Do you know what these sixty words mean? Tick them if you do or look them up to remind yourself.

	Tick here if you know what the word means	Look at this page if you need reminding
absurd		12
accepting		18
ad-lib		18
amphitheatre		23
antagonist		20
anti-hero		20
aside		19
auditorium		16
barndoor		29
blocking		19
centring		19
characterisation		19
chorus		20
climax		20
cross-cutting		24
cross-fade		31
cyclorama		16
dialogue		20
direct address		20
ensemble		83
epilogue		21
flashback		25
forum theatre		25
Fresnel		29
gel		30
genre		21
gobo		30
hubris		21

	Tick here if you know what the word means	Look at this page if you need reminding
improvisation		19
iris		30
melodrama		9
metaphor		21
monologue		21
narration		26
naturalism		10
patch		31
pathetic fallacy		21
plot		21
preset		31
prologue		21
promenade		23
proscenium		23
protagonist		20
proxemics		19
rake		16
rigging		31
role		19
set		17
soliloquy		21
stroboscope		29
style		83
stylisation		19
symbol		84
tableau		27
theatre-in-the-round		22
thespian		3
traverse		23
wings		17

Last-minute learner

Skills, techniques and genres

Preparation techniques

actor / designer objectives
breathing exercises
mantle of the expert
mirror exercises
movement exercises
Relaxation exercises
research
role on the wall

Rehearsal techniques

blocking
character modelling
character objectives
emotional memory
forum theatre
hot-seating
internal dramatic dialogue
mime
off-text improvisation
on-text improvisation
role reversal
tableaux
thought-tracking
working in units

Performance skills (voice)

accent
addressing the audience
mannerism
pitch
strength / tension
tone
volume

CHECK!

Do you know enough about these to be able to talk and write about them with confidence as well as use them in practice?

Performance skills (body)

circle of attention
facial expression
facing out of the drama
gesture
levels
mannerisms
movement
posture
strength / tension

CHECK!

Have you used these in your practical work? Can you say why you used them and what effects they had on your work?

Group techniques
banners
chorus
counterpoint
flashback
flash-forward
monologue / solo
narration
physical theatre
repetition and echo
slow motion
synchronised movement
use of levels

Technical techniques
drawing plans and diagrams
identifying performance demands
identifying textual demands
knowing the performance space
preparing cue-sheets
recognising technical interdependence
using equipment correctly and safely
using materials successfully

CHECK!

Have you considered how your own work, or work you have seen, fits into the different families or 'genres' of drama?

Performance skills (timing)
awareness of audience
flow
pace
rhythm
pause

CHECK!

When planning and reflecting on your practical work, have you taken account of these techniques?

Most popular genres
comedy
farce
horror
melodrama
pantomime
thriller
tragedy

Other genres	
black comedy	poetic drama
Commedia dell 'arte	romance
fantasy	satire
historical drama	sci-fi
kitchen-sink drama	soap opera
light opera	theatre of the absurd
mime	tragicomedy
musical	whodunnit / detective
period drama	

Key figures in drama

Here are the names and a very few details of some of the figures whose work has been influential in the development of the theatre as we know it today.

Before the Common Era (BCE)	
Thespis (c. 534)	Thespis was the first dramatist to use an actor alongside the chorus.
Famous playwrights in Ancient Greece: • Aeschylus (525–456) • Euripides (480–406) • Sophocles (495–406) • Aristophanes (448–385)	
Aristotle (384–322)	Although Aristotle was not a dramatist himself, he drew up a set of 'rules' for drama that influenced writers for centuries afterwards.
Famous playwrights in Ancient Rome: • Plautus (254–184) • Terence (190–159)	
Common Era (CE)	
James Burbage (1530–1597)	Burbage built the first permanent theatre in London. It was simply called The Theatre. Its timbers were later used to build The Globe.
Famous playwrights in the time of Elizabeth I and James I: • Christopher Marlowe (1564–1593) • Ben Jonson (1572–1637) • William Shakespeare (1564–1616)	
Thomas Killigrew (1612–1683) and William D'Avenant (1606–1668)	Charles II awarded Killigrew and D'Avenant special licenses to perform plays. As a result, their theatre companies were the only ones allowed to perform 'legitimate plays', that is, plays without singing and dancing, for the next century.
Aphra Behn (1640–1689)	The best-known of a number of women playwrights at work during the reign of Charles II. Their work paved the way for later work by women dramatists.
Carlo Goldoni (1707–1793)	An Italian dramatist who drew on the earlier form of Commedia dell'arte and influenced the work of later writers of comedy and farce.

David Garrick (1717–1779)	The greatest actor of his time, Garrick's technique of playing characters as if they really existed was revolutionary.
Sir Henry Irving (1838–1905)	A great actor in the time of Queen Victoria and especially known for his declamatory (that is, 'big') acting style. Irving was the first actor to be knighted.
Dion Boucicault (1822–1890)	A leading writer and director of melodramas, Boucicault helped introduce the laws on copyrighting which stopped work produced by one writer simply being copied by others.
Henrik Ibsen (1828–1906) August Strindberg (1849–1912) Anton Chekhov (1860–1904)	Famous writers associated with naturalisim, a movement which tried to replace the big, over-the-top style of melodrama with something that looked and sounded more true to life.
Konstantin Stanislavski (1863–1938)	A great Russian director who tried to give the illusion of truth and reality in his work. He later influenced the American director Lee Strasberg who formulated what became known as 'the method', a way of training actors to 'become' the characters they were playing.
Edward Gordon Craig (1872–1966)	An influential designer whose ideas have helped shape many modern theatre productions.
Antonin Artaud (1896–1948)	A French actor, poet and director, Artaud was influenced by ritualistic forms of theatre. He strove for symbolism and spirituality. His writing has influenced modern writers and directors such as Steven Berkoff and Peter Brook.
Bertolt Brecht (1898–1956)	A German writer and director, Brecht tried to use theatre to get audiences to think about political and moral issues by rejecting illusion and mimicry.
Samuel Beckett (1906–1989)	Along with Eugène Ionesco and Jean Genet, Beckett is a writer whose work is often associated with the theatre of the absurd which sees mankind's plight as essentially pointless.
Dennis Potter (1935–1994)	Dennis Potter is best known for his innovative work in television drama.
Arthur Miller (1915–2005)	Probably the greatest of American playwrights.